Up & Running
with PageMaker on the Macintosh

Up & Running
with PageMaker®
on the Macintosh®

Craig Danuloff

San Francisco • Paris • Düsseldorf • Soest

Acquisitions Editor: Dianne King
Series Editor: Joanne Cuthbertson
Editor: Judith Ziajka
Technical Editor: Jeff Green
Production Editor: Carolina Montilla
Word Processors: Lisa Mitchell, Paul Erickson
Book Designer: Elke Hermanowski
Icon Designer: Helen Bruno
Screen Graphics: Brendan Fletcher, Delia Brown
Desktop Production Artist: Helen Bruno
Proofreader: Dina F. Quan
Cover Designer: Archer Designs

Library of Congress Card Number: 90-71028
ISBN: 0-89588-695-2

Manufactured in the United States of America
10 9 8 7 6 5 4

Up & Running

Let's say that you are comfortable with your PC. You know the basic functions of word processing, spreadsheets, and database management. In short, you are a committed and eager PC user who would like to gain familiarity with several popular programs as quickly as possible. The Up & Running series of books from SYBEX has been developed for you.

Who this book is for

This clearly structured guide shows you in 20 steps what the product can do, how you make it work, and how soon you can achieve practical results.

What this book provides

Your Up & Running book thus satisfies two needs: It describes the program's capabilities, and it lets you quickly get acquainted with the program's operation. This provides valuable help for a purchase decision, along with a 20-step basic course that will give you a solid foundation in the program—even if you're a beginner with scant prior knowledge.

The benefits are plain to see. First, you invest in software that meets your needs because, thanks to the appropriate Up & Running book, you will know the program's features and limitations. Second, once you purchase the product, you can skip the instruction manual and learn the basics of the program by following the 20 steps.

We have structured the Up & Running books so that the busy user spends little time studying documentation and so that the beginner is not burdened with unnecessary text.

Structure of the book

A clock shows your work time for each step. This indicates how much time you can expect to spend on each step with your computer.

Required
time

   **Clock**

Naturally, you'll need much less time if you only read the steps rather than carrying them out at your computer. You can also save some time by scanning the short notes in the margins to find the most important sections within a step.

Three symbols are used to highlight points of special note. These symbols and their meanings are shown below:

Symbols

Action

Tip

Warning

An Up & Running book cannot, of course, replace a book or manual containing advanced applications. However, you do receive the information needed to put the program to practical use and to learn its basic functions.

The first step always covers software installation in relation to hardware requirements. You'll learn how to operate the program with your available hardware. Various methods for starting the program are also explained.

Contents

The second step introduces the program's user interface.

The remaining 18 steps demonstrate basic functions, using examples or short descriptions. You also learn about various facilities for formatting text, importing text and graphics, and using style sheets and master pages. The last steps cover special program features, such as creating indexes and files and using the table editor.

Steps 3–20

Now you see how an Up & Running book will save you time and money.

SYBEX is very interested in your reaction to the Up & Running series. Your opinions and suggestions help all readers, and thereby help you.

Table of Contents

Before using PageMaker 4.0, you must install the program on your hard disk. The process of installing PageMaker allows you to specify the type of text files you will be importing into your PageMaker publications, the printers you will be using, and whether or not you will be using the templates and Getting Started files Aldus provides.

Hardware Requirements

The minimum hardware required to use PageMaker 4.0 is a Macintosh Plus computer with 1 megabyte of RAM and a hard disk. The recommended hardware, however, is a Macintosh SE or SE/30 or a Macintosh II (II, IIx, IIcx, IIci, or IIfx) with at least 2 megabytes of RAM and a hard disk with at least 40 megabytes of storage space.

PageMaker can utilize any monitor that is attached to your Macintosh, though you can gain advantages by using a full-page display or two-page display monitor. PageMaker takes full advantage of color monitors and supports 8-bit, 16-bit, and 24-bit color display modes.

Your Macintosh should use Apple System Software version 6.03 or higher. To check your System Software version, choose the About the Finder command from the Finder's Apple menu.

PageMaker works best with PostScript laser printers such as the Apple LaserWriter II NT or LaserWriter II NTX, but it also supports QuickDraw laser printers such as the Apple LaserWriter II SC.

Hard Drive Space

To install PageMaker, you need at least 4.2 megabytes of free space on your hard drive. If you want to install PageMaker plus all of the template and tutorial files included on the PageMaker disks, you will need a total of 5.3 megabytes of free space. If you do not have enough free space available, you will have to delete some of the files on your hard drive to create enough free space to install PageMaker.

Installing PageMaker 4.0

To begin the installation of PageMaker 4.0, insert Disk 1 into your Macintosh and double-click on the Aldus Installer utility, which is in the Utilities folder. The Aldus Installer main window will then appear. By default, the installer automatically selects all three installation options. If you do not want to install the template files or the Getting Started files (which are used in conjunction with the tutorial in the *Tutorial* manual that accompanies PageMaker), deselect these options. Click the Install button to begin the installation.

The Aldus APD Installation dialog box appears next. If you know which printers you will be using to print your publications, select the corresponding APD files and click the OK button. If you are unsure which printers you will be using, click the Select All button and then click the OK button. The Aldus Filters Installation dialog box appears next. Use the Select All button to choose all of the available filters and then click the OK button to proceed. When the Aldus Language Installation dialog box appears, click English option in the Available window, click the Install button, and then click the OK button.

In the Aldus Personalization dialog box, enter your name, your company name, and the serial number that appears on the bottom of your PageMaker box. Click the OK button to display a verification dialog box and then confirm your entries by clicking the OK button again.

You are now ready to select the folder into which PageMaker 4.0 will be installed. Use the Drive button and the scrolling window in the Designate Folder dialog box (see Figure 1.1) to select the folder into which you want PageMaker installed. The lower-left corner of the dialog box will confirm that your drive has enough free space to install PageMaker. If you do not have enough space, you will have to click the Cancel button, quit the Aldus Installer utility, create more free space on your hard drive, and then begin again.

Click the OK button to begin the installation. As the installation proceeds, you will be prompted to insert Disks 2, 3, and 4. During the installation, a PageMaker 4.0 folder will be created, and the PageMaker 4.0 application and several associated files will be placed in this folder. An Aldus folder, containing other files that PageMaker needs, will be placed in your System folder.

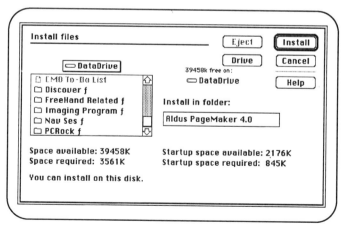

Figure 1.1: The Install files dialog box

This step describes the PageMaker user interface, which you use to control PageMaker and create your publications. As with other Macintosh applications, PageMaker presents commands in menus, options in dialog boxes, and tools on floating palettes. PageMaker also supports numerous keyboard shortcuts.

Menus and Commands

PageMaker menus have three types of commands, illustrated in Figure 2.1:

- Executing commands. These commands perform some action immediately upon being selected. Examples are the Close, Quit, and Paste commands.

- Toggling commands. These commands control options that are turned on and off each time the command is chosen. A checkmark appears before the name of a toggling command when the option is turned on.

- Ellipses commands. Selecting a command that ends with an ellipsis, such as Create Index... or Type Specifications..., displays a dialog box. The dialog box presents additional options.

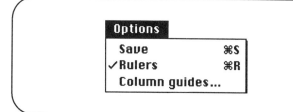

Figure 2.1: A fictitious menu containing one executing command, one toggling command, and one ellipsis command

Dialog Boxes

PageMaker dialog boxes offer four types of options, illustrated in Figure 2.2:

- Radio button options. These options are preceded by small round buttons and usually appear in groups. You can select only one radio button option in a group at one time.

- Check box options. These options are preceded by a small square button and also tend to appear in groups. You can select any number of check boxes in a group.

- Option box options. Option boxes are used to enter text that specifies the value of an option. Clicking an option box produces a flashing insertion point cursor, where you can then type your entry.

- Buttons. The most common buttons found in dialog boxes are the OK button (which closes the dialog box

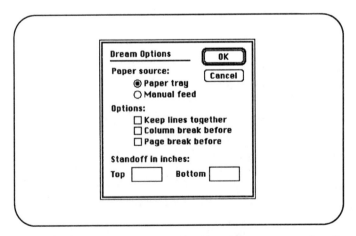

Figure 2.2: A fictitious dialog box containing one set of radio button options, one set of check box options, an option box, and some buttons

and executes the selected options) and the Cancel button (which close the dialog box and reverts all options to their previous settings). But there are other buttons, too. Some have ellipses; clicking these displays additional dialog boxes.

Tools

PageMaker provides eight tools on a floating toolbox palette (Figure 2.3). You use these tools to create new text and graphic elements and to modify imported elements. You can reposition the toolbox by dragging it by its title bar, and you can toggle the toolbox display off and on using the Toolbox command in the Windows menu or by pressing Command-G. The eight tools are as follows:

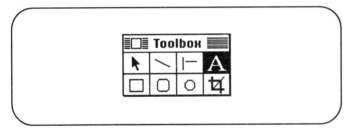

Figure 2.3: The PageMaker toolbox

- The arrow tool. Use this tool to select, reposition, and resize text and graphic elements.

- The diagonal-line tool. Use this tool to draw lines in PageMaker. With the diagonal-line tool, you can create lines at any angle. To control the weight of lines drawn with this tool, use the Lines command in the Element menu.

  Holding down the Shift key while drawing with the di-agonal-line tool allows you to draw lines only at 90° or 45° angles.

- The perpendicular-line tool. Use this tool to draw lines at 90° or 45° angles. To control the weight of lines drawn with this tool, use the Lines command in the Element menu.

- The text tool. Use this tool to create new text in Page-Maker or to edit new text that has been imported into PageMaker.

- The square-corner tool. Use this tool to draw squares and rectangles. To control the weight of the shape drawn with this tool, use the Lines command. To control the fill used in the shape, use the Fill command.

  Holding down the Shift key while drawing with the square-corner tool constrains the shape to a perfect square.

- The rounded-corner tool. Use this tool to draw rounded squares and rectangles. To control the weight of the shape drawn with this tool, use the Lines command. To control the fill used in the shape, use the Fill command.

  Holding down the Shift key while drawing with the rounded-corner tool constrains the shape to a perfect square.

- The circle/oval tool. Use this tool to draw circles and ovals. To control the weight of the shape drawn with this tool, use the Lines command. To control the fill used in this shape, use the Fill command.

  Holding down the Shift key while drawing with the circle/oval tool constrains the shape to a perfect circle.

- The cropping tool. Use this tool to crop imported graphics.

Cursors

As you use PageMaker, the shape of the mouse cursor changes, depending on the tool you have chosen or the key you are pressing. PageMaker uses the following cursors, shown in Figure 2.4.

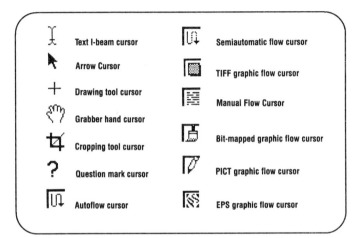

Figure 2.4: The cursors seen in PageMaker

- Arrow cursor. This cursor appears when the arrow tool is selected, or when any other tool is selected and the mouse is positioned over the menu bar, scroll bars, or palettes.

- Text I-beam cursor. This cursor appears when the text tool is selected.

- Drawing tool cursor. This cursor appears when the diagonal-line tool, perpendicular-line tool, square-corner tool, rounded corner tool, or circle/oval tool is selected.

- Grabber-hand cursor. This cursor appears when you press the Option key and hold down the mouse button. The cursor also appears when you hold down the mouse button while the cropping tool is positioned on top of a graphic.

- Cropping tool cursor. This cursor appears when the cropping tool is selected.

- Question mark cursor. This cursor appears when you press Command-? or press the Help button on the extended keyboard.

- Flow-icon cursors. The text-flow icons (that represent the Autoflow, Semiautomatic Flow, Manual Flow, Paint Graphic, PICT Graphic, EPS Graphic, and TIFF graphics selections) appear after a file has been selected and imported using the Place... command.

Keyboard Shortcuts

PageMaker offers keyboard shortcut commands for most of its menu commands, as well as for many of the options found in various PageMaker dialog boxes. You can execute these keyboard shortcuts at any time.

The Publication Window

This step introduces an important aspect of PageMaker: the publication window, the on-screen area in which you build your documents and access PageMaker's layout tools. You can have only one PageMaker publication open at any one time, so only one publication window can be open.

Window Elements

Exactly what you see in the publication window depends on the options you select while using PageMaker and the commands you use to manipulate the display. Figure 3.1 shows the most common elements displayed in the publication window.

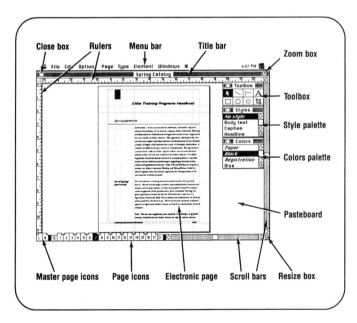

Figure 3.1: The PageMaker publication window

- The *menu bar* contains the Apple menu plus the seven menus that contain the PageMaker commands.

- The *title bar* identifies the current publication by listing the name with which it was last saved to disk. If the current publication is new and has not been saved, it is named *Untitled*.

- The *close box* is used to close the current publication window. Clicking this box is the same as choosing the Close command from the File menu.

- The *zoom box* is used to quickly change the size of the publication window. Clicking the zoom box toggles the window size between its maximum size and a smaller size that you define.

- The horizontal and vertical *rulers* allow you to accurately position elements on your publication pages and to measure the distance between two items.

- The *electronic page* represents one page of your publication. (You'll learn later how to view two electronic pages at once.) This page can be viewed at eight different view sizes (magnifications and reductions), as discussed later in this step. Positioning text and graphic elements on electronic pages is the essence of using PageMaker.

- The *pasteboard* is the empty area that surrounds the electronic page. The pasteboard acts like a work area where you can temporarily store text or graphic elements until you decide to position them on one of the electronic pages in your publication.

- *Page icons* are used to select the pages that are displayed in the publication window. One page icon is provided for each page in your publication. Clicking a page icon displays that page in the publication window. Page icons labeled L and R represent the left and right master pages.

- The vertical and horizontal *scroll bars* are used to change the portion of the electronic page and pasteboard that is displayed in the publication window. You can use the scroll bars by clicking the arrows at either end of each bar, by clicking the gray area between the arrows, or by dragging the small white box inside the scroll bars.

- Dragging the *resize box* lets you change the overall size of the publication window. After the window has been resized, all of the contents of the window are redrawn in relation to the new size.

- The *toolbox* contains the eight tools used in creating publications. Clicking any tool selects that tool. You can reposition the toolbox by dragging its title bar, and you can hide the toolbox by clicking its close box. To redisplay a hidden toolbox, choose the Toolbox command from the Windows menu.

- The *Styles* and *Colors* palettes present lists of style sheets and colors that you can apply to the various elements in your publication. You can reposition each of these palettes by dragging the title bar, and you can hide them by clicking the close box. To redisplay a hidden Styles or Color palette, choose the Styles Palette or Colors Palette command from the Windows menu.

View Sizes

When creating, editing, and arranging text and graphic elements on publications pages, you must choose whether to work with magnified views of the electronic pages or to use actual-size or reduced-size views. Magnified views provide great detail and help you accurately edit text and position elements. However, they let you see only a small portion of one page at one time. Reduced views, in contrast, allow you to see large portions of a page, or even two entire pages, but they make accurately positioning elements and distinguishing small details difficult.

In PageMaker you can quickly and easily move between eight different *view sizes* ranging in magnification from 400 percent enlargement to reductions that display an entire page in just a few square inches. Because you can so easily change view sizes, you can take advantage of enlarged sizes when you need to accurately edit or position an element, and you can switch to a reduced view size when you need to see larger sections of your pages or dramatically reposition elements.

Choosing a view size

PageMaker provides two different ways to change the view size in the publication window:

- You can choose one of the eight view size commands from the Page menu. The command choices are Fit in Window, Fit in World, 25%, 50%, 75%, Actual Size, 200%, and 400%. Figure 3.2 shows the same page viewed at 75% and at 200%.

Hold down the Shift key while selecting Fit in Window to see the eighth view size, Fit in World.

- You can use one of the keyboard–mouse click shortcuts to change the view size. Holding down the Command and Option keys and clicking the mouse button toggles the view size between Fit in Window and Actual Size. Holding down Shift-Command-Option and clicking the mouse button toggles the view size between Actual Size and 200%. In either case, the enlargement or reduction is centered at the position on the page where the mouse is pointing.

You may choose to develop your ow
lum. We reserve the right to review
curriculum for accuracy and content
may ask you to revise the materials i
be used to teach an approved class
Agreement, Section 2.4 (b)] Please submit your curriculum to
before your first scheduled class We'll review your materials

curriculum for

may ask you to

be used to teac]

1t, Section 2.4 (b)] Please subm:

ur first scheduled class. We'll re

Figure 3.2: Portions of the same page viewed at 75% and at 200%

Scrolling the Display

The range of view sizes provided in PageMaker require you
frequently to adjust the portion of your page that is currently
being viewed. You can make this adjustment in several ways:

- You can use the scroll bars located on the bottom and
  right edges of the publication window. You can manipulate the scroll bars by clicking the white arrows, by
  clicking the gray area between the arrows, or by dragging the white box within the scroll bars.

- You can access the grabber hand by pressing the Option key and then holding down the mouse button. Moving the mouse while the grabber hand is displayed pushes the current page around the publication widow.

- As already mentioned, PageMaker centers the display at the location to which the arrow cursor points when the view size is changed using keyboard–mouse click shortcuts. Often the easiest way to reposition the display is to change to the Fit in Window view with the Command-Option–mouse click command. Then point to the area you want displayed and change to actual or 200% size using, respectively, Command-Option–mouse click or Shift-Command-Option–mouse click.

Turning the Page

Although a single PageMaker publication can be up to 999 pages long, the publication window displays only one or two pages at once. The page icons in the lower-left corner of the publication window represent pages in the current publication. Each page icon contains the number of the page it represents. The icon of the page currently being displayed is highlighted (filled with black), as shown in Figure 3.3.

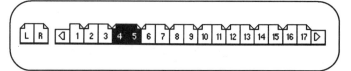

Figure 3.3: The page icons in the lower-left corner of the publication window

You can move between pages in three ways:

- You can point to the page icon of the page you want to turn to and click the mouse button. When not all of the page icons fit on the display, arrows are added to the left and right of the page icons. Click these arrows to scroll the page icons and find other pages in your publication.

If you hold down the Shift key while clicking a page icon, PageMaker turns to the page you have selected and uses the Fit in Window view to display the page. If you do not hold down the Shift key, the page is displayed in whatever view size was last used to display it.

- You can press Command-Tab to turn to the next page or press Shift-Command-Tab to turn to the previous page. As the page is turned, the page icons of the displayed pages are automatically highlighted.

- You can select the Go to Page command from the Page menu, enter the number of the page you want to turn to, and click on OK.

To turn more than one page at a time, press the Command–key sequence once for each page turn you want to make. For example, to turn forward three pages, press Command-Tab three times.

In this step, you start using PageMaker. You will learn how to create new publication files, open publication files that have previously been saved to disk, save your work, and end a PageMaker work session.

If you are experienced with the Macintosh, most aspects of the functions discussed in this chapter will be familiar to you. Some aspects of these procedures are unique to PageMaker, however, so even experienced Macintosh users should read this step.

Creating New Publications

As in almost all Macintosh applications, you create new PageMaker files (called *publications*) by choosing the New command from the File menu. PageMaker allows only one publication to be open at once, so the New command is dimmed if a publication is already open. You have to close an open publication using the Close command before you can access the New command.

After you choose the New command, the Page Setup dialog box (Figure 4.1) appears. The options in this dialog box specify the basic characteristics of the pages in your publication.

1. Select a page size from the Page option pop-up menu. To use a nonstandard page size, choose Custom from the pop-up menu and then enter values in the Page Dimensions option boxes.

2. If you want the first page of your publication numbered with a page number other than 1, enter that number in the Start Page # option box.

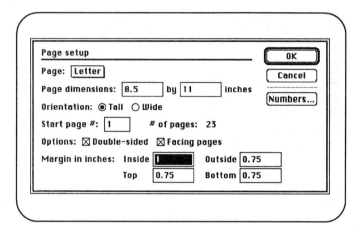

Figure 4.1: The Page Setup dialog box

3. If you know how many pages your publication will include, enter that value in the # of Pages option box. If
   you are unsure how many pages you will need, just
   enter the minimum number of pages you will need; you
   can add additional pages later.

4. Check the Double-Sided option if the publication you
   are creating will be double-sided and you want to be
   able to specify different column arrangements or repeating elements (such as running heads and page
   numbers) for left and right pages. Check the Facing
   Pages option if you will be working on a double-
   sided publication and want to see left and right pages
   together on the screen.

5. Enter values in the four Margin options to define the
   margins of your publication pages.

When you are satisfied with the Page Setup dialog box options, press the Enter or Return key or click the OK button.
PageMaker will then create your new publication and open a
new publication window on the screen.

Opening Publications

To open a publication file that has been saved on disk, choose the Open command from the File menu. PageMaker allows only one publication to be open at once, so the Open command is dimmed if a publication is already open, and you will have to close that publication using the Close command before you can access the Open command.

After you choose the Open command, a standard file dialog box (Figure 4.2) appears. Use the Drive button and folder bar to navigate your disks; then select the name of the file you want to open. Click the OK button or double-click the file name to open the file.

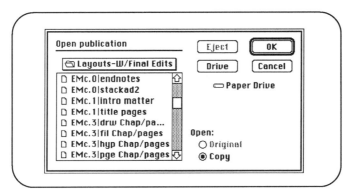

Figure 4.2: The Open Publication dialog box

Saving Publications

While working on your publication, you should frequently save your work by choosing the Save command from the File menu. The keyboard equivalent of the Save command is Command-S.

When the Save command is executed, the version of your publication that is stored on disk is updated to include the current status of your publication. If you want to save your file to a different disk or folder, or if you want to save your publication with a different file name, use the Save As command described later in this step. (The Save As command is automatically used when you execute the Save command for an untitled publication.)

Each time you turn a page in your publication, PageMaker automatically performs a mini-save. This mini-save operation does not modify your disk file, but it allows PageMaker to avoid excessive data loss in the case of a system failure. The mini-save operation also allows you to undo work done since the last page turn by holding down the Shift key while choosing the Revert command from the File menu. You should not, however, rely too heavily on the mini-save. Save your work often using the normal Save command.

The Save As Command

As in other Macintosh applications, you use the PageMaker Save As command to save your file to a different disk or folder or to save a new version of your publication with a different file name.

A unique aspect of the PageMaker Save As command is that publications saved with the Save As command are 30 to 50 percent smaller than those saved using the Save command. For this reason, you should occasionally use the Save As command to compress your files.

Although you can use the Save As command to overwrite the current file by choosing the Save As command but not changing the file name or location, it is recommended that you always give a new file name or version number to files saved with the Save As command. This procedure will multiply the number of files on your disk and therefore require you later to

manually delete outdated versions of your files, but it eliminates any danger of your file being ruined by an error during
the Save As operation.

Closing Publications

To close the current publication, choose the Close command
from the File menu. If any unsaved changes have been made
in the publication, a dialog box appears (Figure 4.3) asking if
you want to save the changes that have been made.

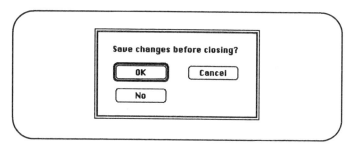

Figure 4.3: The Save Changes before Closing dialog box

Click the Yes button or press the Enter or Return key to save
your work and update the current disk file. Clicking the No
button causes the unsaved changes made to the publication to
be lost permanently. Clicking the Cancel button returns you
to the publication window, where you can continue working
or execute the Save As command to select a new file name or
storage location.

Quitting PageMaker

Quit PageMaker by choosing the Quit command from the File
menu. If unsaved changes have been made in the publication,
the Save Changes? dialog box appears, offering the options
described earlier in this step. If no unsaved changes exist,
PageMaker quits.

In this step you begin to create an actual publication, designing the layout grid into which you will later place the text and graphic elements of your publications.

A layout grid consists of column guides and vertical and horizontal ruler guides. Positioning these guidelines, and using PageMaker's rulers, helps you accurately position elements on your publication pages and ensures that your layout is consistent. However, you can change or ignore these guidelines at any time and freely exercise your creative powers. The range and combinations of grids you can create is limitless. After you finish this step, you may want to spend additional time experimenting further.

Column Guides

The first decision you will usually make about the design of a new publication is the number of columns each page will use. To specify columns, you use the Column Guides command in the Options menu. Choose this command to display the Column Guides dialog box, shown in Figure 5.1.

> **Column guides**
>
> | | Left | Right | | OK |
> |---|---|---|---|---|
> | Number of columns: | 3 | 1 | | Cancel |
> | Space between columns: | .0457 | 0.167 | inches | |
>
> ☒ Set left and right pages separately

Figure 5.1: The Column Guides dialog box as it appears when you use the facing pages

If your publication does not use the Facing Pages option, the screen displays only one set of option boxes. If you are using the Facing Pages option and you want to set a different number of columns on your left and right pages, select the Set Left and Right Pages Separately option, and left and right column options will appear separately.

In these option boxes, enter the number of columns you want your pages to use and the amount of space you want between your columns. You can specify up to 10 columns per page, with column spacing as large as 1 inch. Click the OK button to close the dialog box and create the column guides. Column guides appear as dashed vertical lines. Figure 5.2 shows facing pages each set up with three columns.

Using the arrow tool, you can reposition column guides by dragging them, thereby creating unequal column widths. On

Figure 5.2: Left page using the standard three-columns format and the right page using a customized three-column format

the page on the right in Figure 5.2, the column guides are re-positioned to create three unequal columns. Experiment with different numbers of columns and with column-guide customization. Try dragging the column guides that overlap the page margins, or try dragging the column guides that appear in the middle of the pages.

Once you add text and graphic elements to your pages, you can continue to change the number and position of column guides using the Column Guides command and by dragging the column guides with the arrow tool. This procedure lets you create custom layouts like the one shown in Figure 5.3.

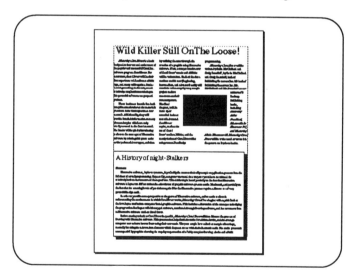

Figure 5.3: A layout created by first defining a three-column layout and adding the upper text and then changing to a one-column layout and adding the lower text

Rulers

PageMaker's rulers let you easily position any element on your pages with a high degree of accuracy. Ruler display is controlled by the Rulers command in the Options menu. You set the units of measure displayed on the rulers in the Preferences dialog box (Figure 5.4), which you access with the Preferences command found in the Edit menu. Set the Measurement System option to control the measurement system used by the horizontal ruler; set the Vertical Ruler option to control the measurement system shown in the vertical ruler.

PageMaker's rulers adjust their display as you change view sizes. The more you zoom in on your page (using the Actual Size, 200%, and 400% View commands), the more detail the ruler provides (see Figure 5.5). When the rulers are turned on, notice that PageMaker tracks the position of the cursor with a small dotted line in both the horizontal and vertical rulers. As your mouse moves, this line shows you your position on the ruler.

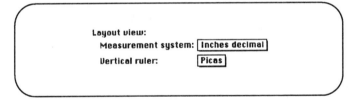

Figure 5.4: Options in the Preferences dialog box, used to specify the units of measurement on PageMaker rulers

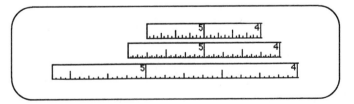

Figure 5.5: Ruler tick marks showing 1/16 units for 75% view, but 1/32 unit for Actual Size and 200% views

Selecting the Snap to Rulers command in the Options menu causes any objects you move to automatically position themselves at the nearest ruler tick mark. Basically, this command creates a magnetic grid that helps you align and position objects. Because more tick marks are displayed at the more magnified view sizes, you can position objects more accurately when working at 200% view than at actual size.

By default, the zero point of horizontal and vertical rulers is positioned at the upper-left corner of documents that do not use the Facing Pages option; the zero point is on the margin between the left and right pages, at the top edge, when the Facing Pages option is in effect. The position of the zero point is critical, because it determines the relative position of all measurements made using the rulers. To reset the zero point, do the following:

1. Point the arrow cursor to the crosshair in the upper-left corner of the publication window, where the horizontal and vertical rulers meet.

2. Click and hold down the mouse button.

3. Drag the zero point to the position on the page that you want set as 0,0.

4. Release the mouse button.

Ruler Guides

In addition to column guides and ruler tick marks, PageMaker provides one more tool that helps you to define your pages and accurately position page elements: ruler guides. Ruler guides are nonprinting lines that you can freely create, reposition, and remove to mark positions on your pages. You can create up to 40 ruler guides on each page of your publication.

To create a ruler guide,

1. Position the cursor in the horizontal ruler if you want to create a horizontal ruler guide, or in the vertical ruler if you want to create a vertical ruler guide.

2. Press and hold down the mouse button.

3. Drag the cursor onto the publication page, positioning the new ruler guide as desired.

Once ruler guides are in place, you can reposition them by dragging them with the arrow tool. To remove a ruler guide, drag it back into the ruler itself and release the mouse button.

The Guides option in the Preferences dialog box determines whether ruler guides are in front of or behind the other elements on your pages and thereby controls how easy or hard it is to select guides when they overlap text or graphic objects. If you find yourself selecting ruler guides accidentally when you are trying to select text or graphic elements, hold down the Command key; ruler guides will not be selected.

The page shown in Figure 5.6 shows a number of ruler guides to help align graphic objects and determine the position of key page elements.

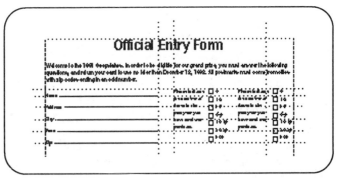

Figure 5.6: A layout using both vertical and horizontal ruler guides

Almost every PageMaker publication will contain text or graphic elements, or a design grid, that repeats on most or all of the publication pages. This step describes how to use *master pages* to control repeating items. Master pages save time and improve the consistency of your documents.

Understanding Master Pages

To the left of the small page icons at the bottom of the publication window are page icons labeled L and R. These icons represent PageMaker's master pages. To begin working on your master pages, click the arrow tool on the right or left master page icon, and PageMaker will turn to the selected master page(s). If you are using the double-sided and facing pages options, both the left and right master page icons will be selected, and both master pages will appear in your display.

*Creating
left and
right
master
pages*

Any text or graphic elements that you add to a master page will automatically appear on each corresponding publication page. (Elements added to the left master page will appear on each left page in the publication, and elements added to the right master page will appear on each right page in the publication.) You cannot print master pages, and the program does not give them page numbers.

Usually, you will want to set your design grid on the master pages, specifying the column guides and ruler guides that will be used on most or all of the pages in your publication. Text and graphic elements that repeat throughout publications, such as lines at the top or bottom of each page, logos, and page numbers, are also added to the master pages. Figure 6.1 shows a typical master page containing column guides, ruler guides, and a page number.

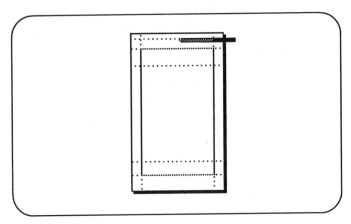

Figure 6.1: A typical master page

Creating a Sample Master Page

To practice using the column guides and ruler guides introduced in Step 5 and to get a better idea of how master pages
are used, follow the steps to create the example master
page shown in Figure 6.1. You will have to scroll the display
and perhaps change view sizes (see Step 3) to complete
these tasks.

1. Click the right master page icon in the lower-left corner of your publication window to turn to the master
   page. (Use the Page Setup command to turn off the
   Double-Sided option if your practice document is
   double-sided.)

2. Choose the Column Guides command from the Options menu. Enter **3** in the Number of Columns option
   and **.75i** in the Space Between Columns option. Then
   click the OK button or press the Return key.

   The measurement system PageMaker uses by default is
   set using the Preferences command in the Edit menu.

You can override the default unit of measure by entering **i** for inches, **p** for picas, **c** for ciceros, or **m** for millimeters in any measurement value. For example, if the dialog box asks for a measurement in inches and your specification is given in picas, you can enter the value 10p6, and PageMaker will apply the option as 10-picas 6 points.

3. Make sure that the zero point of your rulers is at the upper-left corner of the master page. If it is not, reset it by dragging the zero point from the upper-left corner of the screen, where the two rulers meet, and releasing it at the upper-left corner of the page.

4. Drag a ruler guide out of the upper ruler and position it 7 inches from the top of the page.

5. Click the horizontal line tool and draw a line on top of the horizontal ruler guide you just positioned at the 7-inch mark. This line should start and end below the right and left margins of your page.

6. Click the text tool, position the I-beam cursor about ¼inch below your horizontal line near the right margin, and click the mouse button. Type the word **Page**, and then press Command-Option-P. This will produce an "RM," which is the page numbering marker for right master pages.

7. To see how your new master page items appear on normal publication pages, click the page 1 icon in the lower-left corner of the publication window. All of the elements you just added to your master page will now appear on page 1 and on every other right-hand page in your publication.

To add page numbers, set the text cursor and press Command-Option-P

Working with Master Page Elements

While working on regular publication pages, you can reposition column guides or ruler guides provided by the master page simply by dragging them with the arrow tool. These movements affect the guide positions for the current page only; they do not modify the master guides or the position of the guides on any other publication pages.

You cannot directly modify any master page text or graphics that appear on publication pages. To modify these, you must turn back to the master page itself. You can, however, remove all of the master page elements that appear on a publication page, or "hide" some of these elements, as described in the next section.

Removing Master Elements

The Display Master Items command, located on the Page menu, allows you to toggle on and off the display of all master page elements on a publication page. Column guides and ruler guides are not affected by this command; only the text and graphic elements that have been placed on the corresponding master page.

Hiding Selected Elements

Often you will want to remove one or more of the master page elements from a specific page without removing all of the master page elements. The first page of each chapter of a book, for example, is often distinguished from other book pages by its lack of a page number.

To hide any specific master page element without using the Display Master Items command, which removes all master page elements, you must create an opaque object and cover the element you want to hide. You can do this as follows:

1. Select the rectangle tool from the toolbox. Draw a rectangle that covers the element you want to hide. For example, cover the page number.

2. While the rectangle remains selected, choose the Lines command on the Element menu and select the None option from the hierarchical menu.

3. Choose the Fill command on the Element menu and select the Paper option from the hierarchical menu.

Voila! Your page number—or whatever element you covered —has disappeared. You can use this same technique whenever you need to cover elements that cannot be removed.

Restoring Master Guides

PageMaker has one more command that affects the way you manipulate master page elements as they appear on publication pages. The Copy Master Guides command on the Page menu resets the column and ruler guides on the current page back to the way they appear on the master page. Use this feature after you intentionally or accidentally reposition the guides on the current page. If the guides as they appear on the current page already match those on the master page, the Copy Master Guides command is dimmed.

Importing Text

Step 7 describes how to import text into PageMaker from word processing files or from other PageMaker publications. After you import the text, you can then position the text on the pages of your publications. Importing and positioning text are two of the most fundamental tasks you perform in using PageMaker.

File Formats PageMaker Can Import

You can import text that has been created in almost any popular Macintosh or IBM-compatible word processor or that has already been placed in another PageMaker publication. When PageMaker imports text, text formatting is retained; style sheet information is retained from Microsoft Word files. PageMaker can import the following file formats:

Acta

ASCII

DCA

MS Word 1.05, 3.0, 4.0

MS Works, 1.0, 2.0

PageMaker 4.0

RTF

WriteNow

WordPerfect Mac, PC 4.2, PC 5.0

XyWrite3

Beginning the Import Process

To begin the process of importing text, you use the Place command.

1. Choose the Place command from the File menu. The Place dialog box will then appear, as shown in Figure 7.1. Use this dialog box to select the text file you want to import and to specify import options.

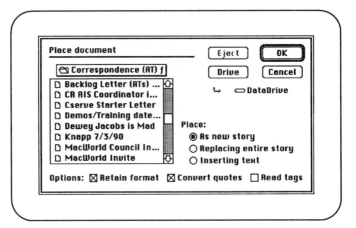

Figure 7.1: The Place dialog box

2. In the scrolling file list, highlight the name of the file you want to import. You can select any text file (in ASCII or a word processing format), or you can select another PageMaker file from which you want to place text, or stories, into the current publication.

3. Click the OK button, or double-click the file name. PageMaker will begin importing the file, and a progress dialog box will appear. If you have selected an ASCII text file, a dialog box containing additional import options will appear.

When importing Microsoft Word 4.0 files, you can access additional import options by holding down the Shift key while clicking the OK button in the Place dialog box. When you import text from another Page-Maker publication, a dialog box displaying a list of available stories will appear. Select the story you want to import and click the OK button.

Positioning Text

After PageMaker has finished reading in the imported file, you can position this text in your publication in any of four ways by using manual text flow, automatic text flow, semi-automatic text flow, or drag placing. Figure 7.2 shows the manual text flow, automatic text flow, and semiautomatic text flow icons.

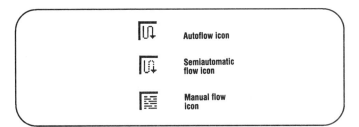

Figure 7.2: Text flow icons

- Manual text flow. Manual text flow is the default method of positioning text. To use this method, you position the manual text flow icon in the upper-left corner of the column in which you want to position your text. Then click the mouse button. The text will flow into the column, stopping at the bottom. If not all of the imported text was placed, a downward arrow will appear in a handlebar at the bottom of the column. Click this downward arrow, and the manual text flow icon will reappear. Position this icon at the top of the next column, turning the page if necessary, and click the mouse button. Repeat this procedure until all the text has been placed.

- Automatic text flow. To use automatic text flow, choose the Autoflow command in the Options menu or hold down the Command key when the manual text flow icon appears. Position the automatic text flow icon at the top of the first column in which you want to position your text. Then click the mouse button. Text will flow until it reaches the bottom of this column, and then it will automatically begin flowing into as many subsequent columns as are needed to position all of the text. PageMaker will turn the pages of your publication and will add new pages if necessary.

To stop automatic text flow before it is completed, click the mouse button.

- Semiautomatic text flow. Holding down the Shift key changes the manual or automatic text flow icons into the semiautomatic text flow icon. Flowing text in semi-automatic mode reloads the text flow icon after each column, but does not initiate further text flow. You must decide where you want the additional text positioned.

To use semiautomatic text flow, press the Shift key, po-sition the semiautomatic text flow icon at the top of the column in which you want to place your text, and click the mouse button. After the column is filled, the man-ual or automatic text flow icon will reappear (unless you are still pressing the Shift key).

To continue flowing text in semiautomatic mode, keep the Shift key depressed and position the icon in another column; then click the mouse button to flow additional text. To flow the remaining text using manual or auto-matic text flow, release the Shift key and toggle the

Autoflow command, or press the Command key, depending on the text flow method you want to use.

• Drag-placing. Use drag-placing to position text when you have not defined column guides for the area in which you want to positon text, or when you want to position text that ignores existing column guides.

To drag-place text, position either the manual or automatic text flow icon at the upper-left corner of the area in which you want to place your text. Press and hold down the mouse button and drag the mouse to create a box that defines the area where you want the text positioned (see Figure 7.3). Release the mouse button, and the text will flow into the area you have defined. If more imported text remains when the area you defined is filled, reload the text flow icon by clicking the downward arrow in the lower handlebar of the new text block. You can then position the remaining text using any of the text flow methods.

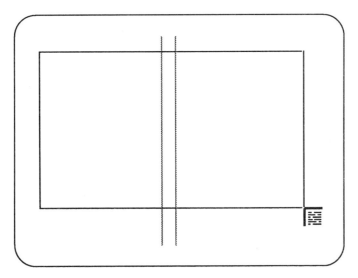

Figure 7.3: Drag-placing imported text

Creating New Text in PageMaker

Although most of the text you use in PageMaker publications will be imported from word processing files, you can also create new text directly in PageMaker. You most often will do this to create small amounts of text such as headlines and captions. If you want to create large amounts of text with PageMaker, you should use the story editor, described later in this book.

Creating small blocks of text

To create small amounts of text, select the text tool from the toolbox. You can create new text blocks inside of existing column guides, on the pasteboard, or you can force a new text block to ignore existing column guides.

To create text within the boundaries of an existing column, position the I-beam cursor inside of the column guides and click the mouse button. The flashing insertion point will then appear at the left margin of the column. Begin typing to create your text block.

To create text outside of existing column guides, position the cursor outside the page margins and click the mouse button. The flashing insertion point will appear, and you can begin typing.

To create a text block that ignores existing column guides, position the cursor at the upper-left corner of the text block you want to define, press and hold the mouse button, drag the mouse to define the size of the text block you want to create, and release the mouse button.

To see the text block you have created, click the arrow tool on top of your new text. You can format and manipulate this text using the procedures described in Steps 8, 9, and 10.

Step 7 described two ways to add text to PageMaker publications. Now it is time to learn more about how PageMaker treats text and how you can manipulate and modify text blocks after they have been created.

Text Blocks

Each unit of text in a PageMaker publication appears within an object called a *text block*. A text block can contain a single word of text or an entire column full of text. A single story, such as an imported word processing file, can flow through a number of different text blocks while still remaining linked as a single story.

A text block is distinguished by the *handlebars* that appear above and below it when you select the text block with the arrow tool or the Select All command. Figure 8.1 shows two selected text blocks. Notice that the tab on the lower handlebar of the text block on the right shows a downward arrow, and the tab on the lower handlebar of the text block on the left shows a plus sign. These symbols indicate that not all of the text from the story the text block contains fits in the selected text block. The downward arrow indicates that the remaining text has not yet been positioned in another text block, and the plus sign indicates that the text continues in another text block.

Handlebars mark the top & bottom of each text block

Manipulating Text Blocks

When you have placed a story that flows through multiple text blocks, you can manipulate the text flow by moving any of the text block handlebars. As Figure 8.2 shows, you can drag the handlebars up or down to shorten or lengthen text blocks.

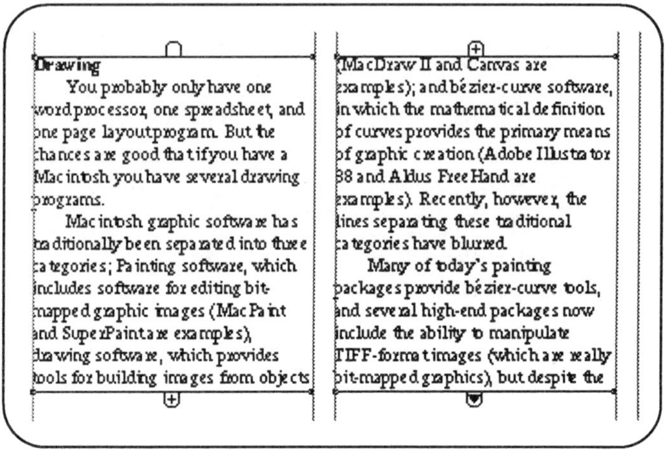

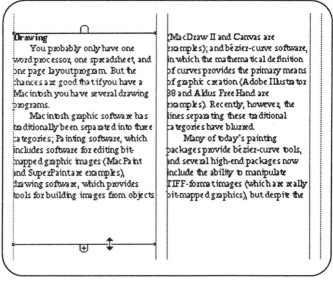

Figure 8.1: Selected text blocks

Figure 8.2: Dragging the handlebar resizes text blocks

- To shorten one text block, select the arrow tool, click the text block so that the handlebars are visible, drag the lower handlebar upward, and release the mouse button. The text that is no longer visible in this text block will appear at the top of the next text block.

- To lengthen a text block, select the arrow tool, click the text block so that the handlebars are visible, drag the lower handlebar downward, and release the mouse button. Text that was previously at the top of the next text block will now appear at the bottom of the current text block.

When you modify the size of text blocks in this way, text flows through all the connected text blocks, no matter how many pages they are on, moving up and down the text blocks.

Repositioning Text Blocks

You can reposition a text block simply by dragging it with the arrow tool. Be careful not to position the arrow on either handlebar, as this will resize the text block rather than reposition it. If you want to move a text block to another page, drag it onto the pasteboard, turn the page, and then drag the block from the pasteboard to its new position. When you move the text block onto the pasteboard, make sure that no part of the text block handlebars touch the electronic page, or the text block will remain with that page.

You can also move text blocks by cutting and pasting them using the commands on the Edit menu.

If you cut and paste a text block that has text connected to other text blocks, the cut and paste process breaks the connection. Text will no longer flow in or out of the text block that was cut and pasted. Text from any text blocks before and after this text block will remain connected as if the cut text block had never existed.

To change the width of a text block, select it with the arrow tool and drag one of the handles that appear on the sides of each handlebar (see Figure 8.3). As you drag, you will see a box that represents the text block size. Release the mouse when this box is the size you want your text block to be. The text will then reflow to fit this new text block size (see Figure 8.3).

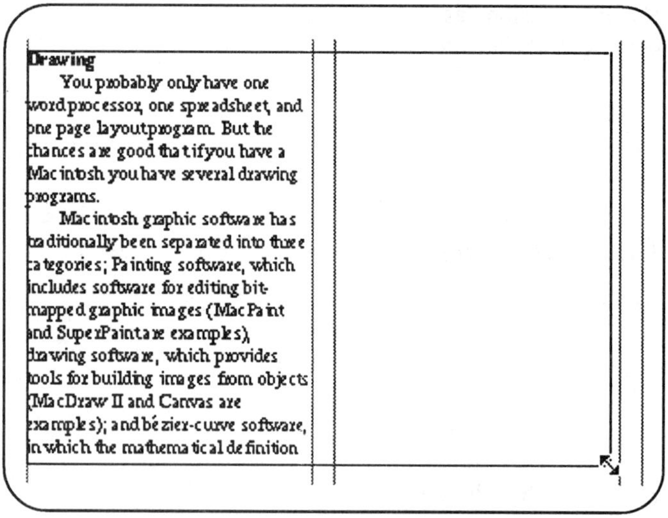

Drawing

You probably only have one word processor, one spreadsheet, and one page layout program. But the chances are good that if you have a Macintosh you have several drawing programs.

Macintosh graphic software has traditionally been separated into three categories; Painting software, which includes software for editing bit-mapped graphic images (MacPaint and SuperPaint are examples), drawing software, which provides tools for building images from objects (MacDraw II and Canvas are examples); and bézier-curve software, in which the mathematical definition

Figure 8.3: Dragging on text block handles resizes text blocks

In this step you will learn about PageMaker's typographic controls. These commands are important because they affect not only the appearance of your publications, but also their readability. PageMaker provides the standard Macintosh controls, such as font, size, leading, and style, with very high levels of precision, as well as advanced control of tracking, kerning, and character spacing.

To learn to use the commands introduced in this step, you should import or create some text and then practice modifying the text format as this step describes.

Character Formatting Basics

Before applying any character formatting commands, you must first select the text you want to modify. (You select text by dragging the text tool over it.) To modify the font, size, leading, width, tracking, or style of your selected type, you can use the appropriate commands from the Type menu, or you can choose the Type Specs command and use the options in the Type Specifications dialog box.

In general, you should use the individual Type menu commands when you want to quickly change a single character attribute, and you should use the Type Specs command when you need to change more than one attribute at one time.

To specify irregular type sizes or leadings, you must either choose the Other... option in the Size or Leading hierarchical menus or choose the Type Specs command and enter the desired value in the Size or Leading option boxes. You can specify type sizes in 0.01-point increments between 1 and 650 points, and you can specify leading in 0.1-point increments between 0 and 1300.

Changing text format from the keyboard

You can use keyboard commands to quickly change the size or style of selected text. Table 9.1 lists the available keyboard equivalents.

Format	Keystroke
Normal Style	Shift-Command-spacebar
Bold	Shift-Command-B
Italic	Shift-Command-I
Underline	Shift-Command-U
Strike-through	Shift-Command-/
Outline	Shift-Command-O
Shadow	Shift-Command-W
Next larger type size	Command-Shift->
Next smaller type size	Command-Shift-<
1-point smaller type	Command-Option-Shift-<
1-point larger type	Command-Option-Shift->

Table 9.1: Keyboard Equivalents for Text Formatting Commands

Setting Character Width

Use PageMaker's Set Width command on the Type menu to compress or expand selected type. Figure 9.1 provides examples of text modified with this command. The default compression options are 70%, 80%, and 90%, and the default expansion options are 110%, 120%, and 130%. If you select the Other... option, the Other Character Width dialog box appears, and you can specify any text width between 0.1% and 250% in 0.1% increments.

Use the Set Width command to achieve special visual effects, not to force text fill a certain space. If you need to modify

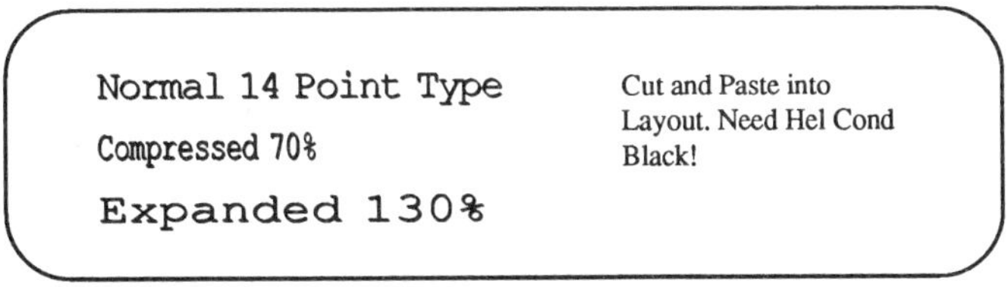

Normal 14 Point Type

Compressed 70%

Expanded 130%

Cut and Paste into
Layout. Need Hel Cond
Black!

Figure 9.1: Examples of type modified with the Character Width command

text for a better fit, use the kerning and tracking commands discussed next.

Kerning

For every character (including letters, numbers, and special symbols) in every Macintosh font, a font designer has predetermined the amount of space that PageMaker will place before and after each character. In most cases, this predetermined character spacing is adequate, but sometimes you may want to modify character spacing.

- In larger type sizes, the default character spacing often leaves too much space between certain characters.

- Your text will not always fit perfectly into the amount of space your layout provides.

- You may want to achieve special effects for design purposes.

PageMaker provides three different types of commands that modify character spacing. The first group of commands, known as *kerning* commands, allow you to modify the character spacing between specific text characters. *Tracking* commands, discussed later in this step, also modify the character spacing, but are generally used to modify larger ranges of text than kerning commands and do not provide as exacting control as kerning commands. The *character spacing* commands, found in the Spacing dialog box discussed in Step 10, lets you modify even larger ranges of text, such as entire stories.

PageMaker offers five kerning commands, listed in Table 9.2. You execute these commands from the keyboard.

Command	*Keystrokes*
Kern together by 1/100 of an em space	Command-Shift-Left Arrow or Option-Delete
Kern apart by 1/100 of an em space	Command-Shift-Right Arrow or Option-Shift-Delete
Kern together by 1/25 of an em space	Command-Left Arrow or Command-Delete
Kern apart by 1/100 of an em space	Command-Right Arrow or Command-Shift-Delete
Clear manual kerning	Command-Option-K or Command-Option-Shift-Delete

Table 9.2: Kerning Commands

To execute any of these commands, place the text insertion point between the characters you want to kern, or select a range of text to kern, and then use the keyboard commands listed in Table 9.2. To reset kerning to its default values, use the Clear Manual Kerning command (Command-Option-K).

Your monitor and current view size will affect your ability to see the results of your kerning on the screen, although even in the best situations, the on-screen appearance is only a rough approximation. To see the actual results of any kerning, print your publication on a PostScript printer. In Figure 9.2, the C has been kerned to surround the following letters to create a special effect.

atch the spirit!

Figure 9.2: Special effects created with kerning

Zoom in to 200% or 400% view size to see the effects of manual kerning as it is performed.

In addition to manual kerning, PageMaker provides an automatic Pair Kerning option that you can apply to any text on a paragraph-by-paragraph basis. This command is found in the Spacing dialog box, which you access by choosing the Paragraph command in the Type menu and then pressing the Spacing button. When you use the Pair Kerning option, Page-Maker automatically applies special character spacing to all text that is approximately the specified type size.

Using automatic pair kerning

You should use Pair Kerning as the default option for almost every paragraph in your publications, because it considerably improves the appearance of your type. However, this option often is applied only to text over 12 points because it slows down the screen display.

Tracking

PageMaker's Track command on the Type menu lets you modify the character spacing for large ranges of text, such as paragraphs or entire stories. Tracking performs character spacing manipulations that are based on the point size of the selected text. Thus, the amount of adjustment the various tracking commands make to the character spacing of your text depends on the point sizes of the type to which tracking is applied.

PageMaker's five tracks—Very Tight, Tight, Normal, Loose, and Very Loose—have been designed to modify character spacing while maintaining maximum text legibility. Figure 9.3 shows the effects of the various tracks on a sample sentence.

dolor in hendreit in vulputa te esse vel illum dolore e u	**Very tight**
dolor in hendreit in vulputa te esse vel illum dolore e u	**Tight**
dolor in hendreit in vulputa te esse vel illum	**Normal**
dolor in hendreit in vulputa te esse vel illum	**Loose**
dolor in hendreit in vulputa te esse vel illum	**Very loose**

Figure 9.3: Examples of PageMaker's tracking options

By default, PageMaker applies the No Track Option to all text in your publication. Applying any tracking command, even Normal, alters the character spacing of your text. After applying any of the tracking commands, return your text to its original character spacing by using the No Track command.

Using the Track command is the best way to change the amount of space consumed by text in your publication. If your text is running long, applying the Tight or Very Tight track often will allow you to fit all of the text into the available space. Be careful when applying different Track commands to different stories, because the visual balance of your publication may be disturbed. Whenever possible, apply one Track command to all body text in your publication and one Track command to all headlines.

Step 10

Paragraph Formatting

In this step you will learn to use PageMaker's paragraph formatting commands to control such elements as text alignment, paragraph indents, character spacing, and paragraph rules. You will also learn how to use tabs. As with character formatting, paragraph formatting is best learned by practicing these commands on some sample text.

Controlling Text Alignment

Any paragraph can be set left justified, right justified, fully justified, centered, or force justified using the Alignment commands in the Type menu or the keyboard equivalents listed in Table 10.1. To apply these commands, you must select some or all the paragraphs you want to modify.

You will use the Alignment commands frequently, so you should learn the keyboard shortcuts

Command	Keystroke
Left justification	Command-Shift-L
Right justification	Command-Shift-R
Full justification	Command-Shift-J
Forced justification	Command-Shift-F
Centering	Command-Shift-C

Table 10.1: Keyboard Equivalents for Alignment commands

Keep in mind that PageMaker aligns text relative to the width of the text block, which may or may not be coincident with column or ruler guides. To see the width of the text block, select the text with the arrow tool. If the width of the text block is incorrect, modify the text block width by dragging the handles of the text block handlebar.

Controlling Paragraph Spacing

As with most Macintosh word processors, you can specify the left, right, and first-line margins for each paragraph in your publication. To change the paragraph margins, select the text you want to modify and choose the Paragraph... command from the Type menu. This will display the Paragraph Specifications dialog box, shown in Figure 10.1.

```
┌──────────────────────────────────────────────────────────────┐
│  Paragraph specifications                          [  OK  ]   │
│  ────────────────────────────────────────────                 │
│  Indents:                  Paragraph space:        [ Cancel ] │
│    Left  [.5    ] inches     Before [.0175] inches            │
│    First [.25   ] inches     After  [0    ] inches  [ Rules...]│
│    Right [0     ] inches                            [Spacing...]│
│  Alignment: [Left]              Dictionary: [US English]      │
│  Options:                                                     │
│    ☒ Keep lines together    ☐ Keep with next [0] lines       │
│    ☐ Column break before    ☒ Widow control  [1] lines       │
│    ☐ Page break before      ☒ Orphan control [2] lines       │
│    ☐ Include in table of contents                            │
└──────────────────────────────────────────────────────────────┘
```

Figure 10.1: The Paragraph Specifications dialog box

Use the Before and After spacing options to offset your paragraphs from each other rather than inserting blank lines between paragraphs. The advantages of this method are that you have more precise control over the spacing, and you can more easily later modify or eliminate this spacing.

The Paragraph options save time and prevent simple formatting errors

Setting Paragraph Options

In the lower half of the Paragraph Specifications dialog box are a group of check boxes that let you control how the text in your publication positions itself within the columns and pages of your document. After you select these commands and close the Paragraph Specifications dialog box, the text in your publication is repositioned in accordance with the new option settings.

- The Keep Lines Together option ensures that the selected paragraph is never broken across a column or page; if the entire paragraph does not fit in the current column, it is moved to the top of the next column or page.

- The Keep with Next option lets you specify that 1, 2, or 3 lines after the last line of the current paragraph will appear on the same page as the last line of the current paragraph. If the specified lines will not fit, then the end of the current paragraph is moved to the top of the next column or page. This option often is used to keep introductions together with lists and to keep graphics and figure captions from being separated. After selecting the Keep with Next option, enter 1, 2, or 3 in the option box to specify the number of lines that you want kept together.

- The Column Break Before and Page Break Before options specify that the selected paragraph always move to the top of a new column or page. These options are most often applied to headlines or subheadings.

- The Widow Control and Orphan Control options specify the minimum number of lines from a paragraph that must be kept together at the end of a page or column or at the top of a page or column. If you do not use these options, PageMaker may break a paragraph across two columns so that a single line appears alone on the last line of a column (creating a window) or at the top of a column (creating an orphan). Selecting these options and entering a value of 2 or 3 into the option boxes instructs PageMaker not to leave single text lines alone at the bottom or top of pages.

Using the Widow Control and Orphan Control options adds a professional touch to your publications.

Controlling Character Spacing

Step 9 introduced two ways of modifying character spacing: kerning and tracking. You can also change the amount of space between text characters in PageMaker by modifying the options in the Spacing dialog box, which you access by clicking the Spacing button in the Paragraph Specification dialog box. Figure 10.2 shows the Spacing dialog box.

Word space:			Letter space:		
Minimum	50	%	Minimum	-5	%
Desired	100	%	Desired	0	%
Maximum	200	%	Maximum	25	%

Figure 10.2: The Spacing dialog box

These spacing options allow you to change the amount of space between the letters and words in the currently selected paragraphs by specifying percentages of the normal letter and word spacing. Both the Letter Space and Word Space options have three parts: Minimum, Desired, and Maximum. The Minimum and Maximum options affect only justified text.

The default Word Space settings are Maximum: 50%, Desired: 100%, and Maximum: 200%. These settings cause PageMaker to apply normal word spacing (100%) in most cases, but to range between 50% of normal word spacing and 200% of normal word spacing when justifying text. To tighten the text in your paragraphs, change the Desired Word Space option to a value less than 100%.

Use fairly narrow ranges of values for the Minimum and Maximum Word Space options. The default range of 50% to 200% can cause your text to appear very tight in some places and very loose in others. Reducing the range by entering 75% as the Minimum value and 150% as the Maximum value eliminates most wide variations in word spacing and makes the appearance of your documents more consistent.

If you specify full justification, PageMaker will apply word spacing outside of the boundaries specified by your Minimum and Maximum settings if necessary to fully justify text.

The default Letter Space settings are Minimum: -5% (5% less than normal), Maximum: 25% (25% more than normal), and Desired: 0% (normal letter space). Because changes in letter spacing can dramatically alter the legibility of your text, you should change these options with care. When working with justified type, modify the Minimum and Maximum values to control the amount of character space manipulation used to achieve justification. To tighten or loosen any text, change the value of the Desired option, moving it positive or negative by a few percentages.

Adding Paragraph Rules

You can add lines above or below any paragraph using Page-Maker's paragraph rules option. Paragraph rules are preferable to lines drawn with the horizontal line tool because they remain in place as the paragraph to which they are connected reflows.

You can add lines above or below para-graphs

To specify paragraph rules, select the paragraph to which you want to add lines, choose the Paragraph command from the Type menu, and then click the Rules... button. The Paragraph Rules dialog box contains two sets of options: one to control the attributes of a rule above the paragraph and one to control the attributes of a rule below the paragraph. Using these options, you can specify the line style, color, and width.

To control the distance above or below the paragraph where the paragraph rule is positioned, click the Options... button. Enter values for the Top and Bottom options to specify the exact distance above or below the baseline of the first or last line in the paragraph the paragraph rule is placed.

Holding down the Option key while clicking the OK button closes all of the nested dialog boxes at once.

Using Tabs

Using tabs in PageMaker is much like using tabs in Microsoft Word. If you are familiar with how Word treats tabs, you will have very little problem using them in PageMaker. If you have not used Microsoft Word, a few things about Page-Maker's tabs might take some getting used to, but you will ultimately find them easy to use—and powerful.

To learn how to use tabs, create a new text block and enter three lines of text, each containing three numbers separated by tabs. Select these three lines of text and choose the Indents/Tabs command from the Type menu to display the Indents/Tabs dialog box, shown in Figure 10.3.

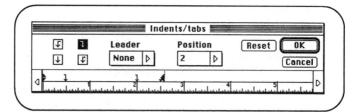

Figure 10.3: The Tabs dialog box

Above the ruler in the Indents/Tabs dialog box are triangles pointing left and right to represent the left and right margins of the selected text block, and triangles pointing downward to represent the default tab stops for the text block. To create a new tab, point your cursor at the position on the ruler where you want the tab and click the mouse button. A new tab icon will appear above the ruler to represent the tab you have created. Create three tabs: one for each of the numbers in each of your lines of text.

You can specify a right, left, center, or decimal tab by clicking the appropriate tab icon before creating your tab, and you can specify a tab leader by using the pop-up menu that appears when you select the Leader option.

Click OK to close the Indents/Tabs dialog box, and the numbers in your sample text block will position themselves according to the tabs you specified. If you are not satisfied with these tab locations, choose the Indents/Tabs command again and adjust the tab markers.

To move a tab, drag the tab icon from one position above the ruler to another. To delete a tab, drag the tab icon from above the ruler completely out of the dialog box and release the mouse button. You can also add, delete, or move tabs by using the pop-up menu that appears when you select the Position option and entering specific values in the Position option box.

You can also use the Indents/Tabs command and dialog box to modify the left, right, and first-line margins of the selected paragraph. To modify these margins, drag the margin triangles on the Indents/Tabs dialog box ruler.

Importing Graphics

This step describes how to import graphics into PageMaker. PageMaker can use virtually any type of Macintosh graphics, including bit-mapped graphics, Encapsulated PostScript graphics, and scanned images. Graphics can be positioned in a fixed location, or they can be set in relation to a specific section of text so that they automatically move if that text is moved.

To learn how to create graphics in PageMaker, see Step 12. To learn various ways to manipulate graphics, see Step 13.

Beginning the Import Process

The Place command was introduced in Step 7, when we discussed how to import text. This same command is used to import graphics, and it is used in almost exactly the same way.

1. Choose the Place command from the File menu.

2. Locate the graphic file you want to import to PageMaker and highlight its name in the scrolling window.

3. Click the OK button or double-click the file name. PageMaker will import the selected graphic.

4. The cursor will change to one of the graphic placement icons shown in Figure 11.1. The type of icon that appears depends on the type of graphic file you have imported.

5. Position the graphic placement icon at the upper-left corner of the place where you want your imported graphic to appear. Then click the mouse button. The graphic will now flow into place.

The Place command is used to import graphics in the same way it was used to import text

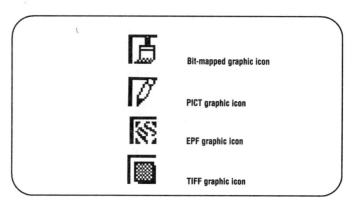

Figure 11.1: The graphic placement icons

You can place graphics using the same drag-placing method you use to place text. With the graphic placement icon displayed, press and hold down the mouse button and drag to create a box representing the size and position you want for your imported graphic. Release the mouse button, and the graphic will appear in the space you have defined. Note that the graphic may be distorted in order to fill the box you have defined. Figure 11.2 shows a placement box being defined with the bit-mapped placement icon.

Types of Graphics

You can import four types of graphic files into PageMaker:

- MacPaint-format files containing bit-mapped images. These are created by many software packages, including painting applications such as MacPaint and Super-Paint, image processing programs, scanning software, and some drawing packages. The majority of clip art you can buy exists in MacPaint-format files.

- PICT-format files containing object-oriented graphic images. These are created by drawing applications

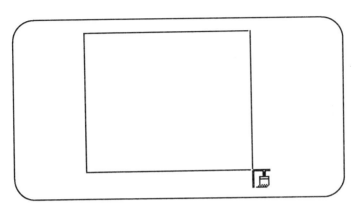

Figure 11.2: Creating a box to drag-place an imported graphic

such as MacDraw II and Canvas, as well as by some scanning software. A few PICT-format clip art packages are available.

- Encapsulated PostScript files (EPS files) containing high-resolution images. These are created by software such as Aldus FreeHand and Adobe Illustrator. Increasingly, clip art is available in this format.

- TIFF (tagged image file format) files containing scanned images. These are created primarily with scanning software, but also with image-editing software such as Adobe PhotoShop and Digital Darkroom.

You can select files of these types in the Place dialog box and import them using the procedure described earlier in this step.

If you have graphic images that are not stored in one of these types of files, you may be able to use those graphics in PageMaker. Any graphic that you can copy to the Macintosh Clipboard or paste into the Macintosh Scrapbook can be transferred into PageMaker. To do this,

1. Open the application that contains the graphic you want to transfer to PageMaker.

2. Select the graphic and choose the Copy command from the Edit menu.

3. Choose Scrapbook DA from the Apple menu and paste the graphic into the Scrapbook with the Paste command. Close the Scrapbook.

4. Quit the application (if you are not using MultiFinder) and launch PageMaker. Open the publication in which you want to insert the graphic.

5. Choose Scrapbook DA from the Apple menu, position the graphic, and choose the Copy command from the Edit menu. Close the Scrapbook.

6. Choose the Paste command from the PageMaker Edit menu.

Independent versus Inline Graphics

Graphics in PageMaker can exist in two forms: as independent graphics or as inline graphics.

Independent graphics can be freely positioned; inline graphics flow along with text

Independent graphics are independent objects, unrelated to any text block—you can move them anywhere on the current page or pasteboard, and they will not move unless you move them. Inline graphics, on the other hand, are embedded in a text block, like graphics you paste into your word processor. Inline graphics cannot be freely moved; they are constrained by their place in the text block. If you change the text above an inline graphic, the graphic will flow to a new position along with the rest of the text in the text block.

Any graphic that can be imported into PageMaker can be either an independent graphic or an inline graphic. You determine how a graphic will be used when you import it, and you can change independent graphics into inline graphics, and vice versa, at any time.

Imported graphics will always be added as independent graphics, unless you select the text tool when you import the graphic. If you set the text cursor within a text block when you import a graphic, you determine whether the imported graphic will be an independent graphic or an inline graphic by selecting the corresponding radio button option in the Place dialog box. Figure 11.3 shows the options as they appear in the Place dialog box when the text cursor has been set in a text block before the Place command was selected.

To create an inline graphic, choose the text tool, set the cursor in an existing text block, and then use the Place command to import a graphic. Leave the As Inline Graphic option selected in the Place dialog box. The imported graphic will be placed at the location of your text cursor.

Inline graphics can be placed on blank lines or on the same lines as text. You can apply paragraph formatting commands to inline graphics to control their margins and their relationship to the text above or below them (using the Keep options). You can select an inline graphic with either the arrow tool or the text tool. Use the arrow tool to select inline graphics when you want to resize them. Use the text tool to select inline graphics when you want to cut or copy them.

To change an inline graphic into an independent graphic, select it with the text tool, choose the Cut command from the

Place:
◉ **As independent graphic**
○ **As inline graphic**
○ Inserting text

Figure 11.3: The Place options

Edit menu, select the arrow tool from the toolbox, and choose the Paste command from the Edit menu.

To change an independent graphic into an inline graphic, select the graphic with the arrow tool, choose the Cut command from the Edit menu, select the text tool from the toolbox, and set the text cursor in the text block where you want the inline graphic to appear. Then choose the Paste command from the Edit menu.

Creating Graphics

This step describes PageMaker's built-in graphic creation tools. You use these tools to create simple graphics, which you can use as design elements for your publication pages. The features and commands in this step are fairly basic, but you will use them almost constantly when working in PageMaker.

The most important aspect of creating lines and shapes is the accuracy with which you position your lines and shapes. Thus, be sure you understand how to use the rulers and ruler guides, introduced in Step 6, and how to change view sizes, introduced in Step 3.

Drawing Lines

The PageMaker toolbox offers two line tools: the horizontal line tool and the diagonal line tool. As mentioned in Step 2, however, using the Shift key with the diagonal line tool forces the diagonal line tool to act like the horizontal line tool. For this reason, you will probably find yourself using the diagonal line tool most frequently.

The diagonal line tool is used most frequently

To draw a line, select one of the the line tools from the toolbox. The cursor will then appear as a crosshair. Position the crosshair at the point where you want to start your new line and press and hold down the mouse button. Drag the mouse to draw the line, releasing the mouse button when the line reaches the required length.

Lines are sometimes called rules, both in the PageMaker program and in the Aldus documentation.

You can use the Line command on the Element menu to change the weight or style of any line created in PageMaker immediately before or after you create it. The Line command provides eight line weights (Hairline, .5 Pt, 1 Pt, 2 Pt, 4 Pt, 6 Pt, 8 Pt, 12 Pt) and nine line styles (Double, Thick-Thin, Thin-Thick, Triple, Thin Dash, Thick Dash, Fat Dash, Square Dot, Round Dot), plus the None and Reverse Line options. Figure 12.1 shows the Line command pop-up menu.

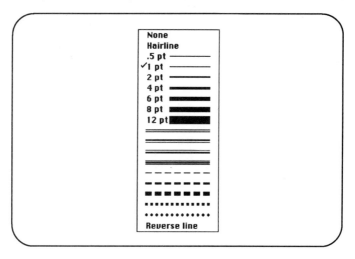

Figure 12.1: The Line command pop-up menu

To change the weight or style of a line after it has been cre-ated, you must select the line. Select lines with the arrow tool. Once selected, lines display handles at each end.

Lines versus Paragraph Rules

As mentioned in Step 10, you can also create lines using the Paragraph Rules dialog box. Paragraph rules are lines above or below text paragraphs. The most important feature of para-graph rules is that they move along with the text paragraphs to which they are assigned. When you need to create lines above or below text, use paragraph rules.

Creating Shapes

The three shape tools in the PageMaker toolbox allow you to create squares, rectangles, circles, and ovals. To draw a new shape, select one of the shape tools from the toolbox. The cursor will then appear as a crosshair. Position the crosshair at the point where you want to start your shape and press and hold down the mouse button. Drag the mouse to draw the shape, releasing the mouse button when the shape reaches the required size.

The shape tools let you create simple squares, rectangles, circles, and ovals

After you have created a shape, use the Line and Fill commands to format it. The Line command was discussed in the section ''Drawing Lines''; the same options can be applied to shapes. The Fill command provides nine shades and eight fill patterns, as shown in Figure 12.2.

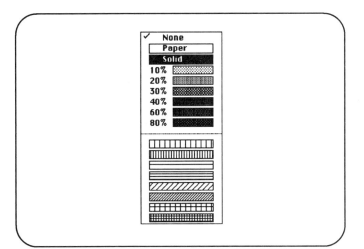

Figure 12.2: The Fill command pop-up menu

Rounding Corners

After creating shapes with the square or rectangle tool, you may want to change the type of corner on the shape. The Rounded Corners command provides six choices that you can apply to any square or rectangle. Figure 12.3 shows the different results that can be achieved using this command.

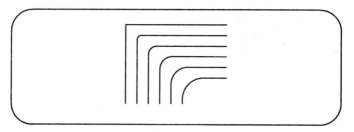

Figure 12.3: The six rounded corners you can create with the Rounded Corners command

To modify the corners on a shape, select the shape with the arrow tool and then choose the Rounded Corners command from the Element menu. The Rounded Corners dialog box will then appear, presenting icons for each of the six corner options. Click the corner you want applied to your shape and then click the OK button to apply your choice and return to the publication window.

Creating Drop Shadow Boxes

One common use for shapes is to create drop shadow boxes. Drop shadow boxes are really two overlapping boxes with text positioned inside of them. To create a drop shadow box,

1. Position your text as required. You may want to reduce the column width of the text slightly to allow space for the drop shadow box.

2. Select the rectangle tool and draw a rectangle around the text. This rectangle should be evenly spaced on all sides of the text. Choose the Hairline or .5 Pt line weight using the Line command and choose Paper fill using the Fill command.

3. Choose the Send to Back command from the Element menu to place the box behind your text.

4. Create another box, starting at the upper-left corner of the text and extending to the lower-right corner, beyond the edge of the first box. Choose the None line weight using the Line command and the 40% fill using the Fill command. Figure 12.4 shows what your drop box will look like at this stage.

5. Choose the Send to Back command from the Element menu to send the shadow box behind the text and the first box. Figure 12.5 shows the resulting drop shadow box.

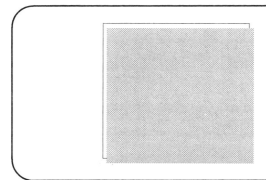

Figure 12.4: A drop shadow box before the second box is sent to the back

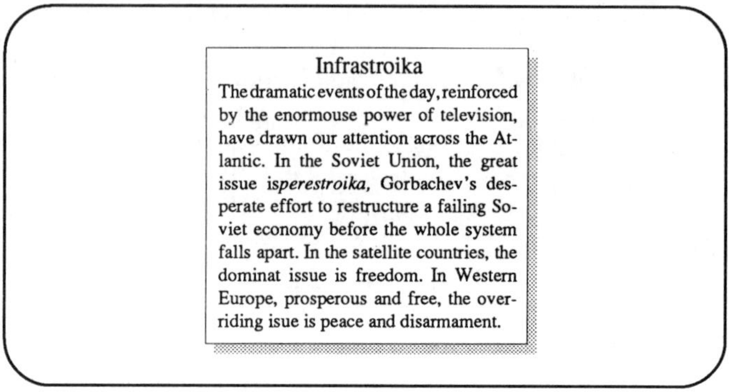

Infrastroika

The dramatic events of the day, reinforced by the enormouse power of television, have drawn our attention across the Atlantic. In the Soviet Union, the great issue is *perestroika,* Gorbachev's desperate effort to restructure a failing Soviet economy before the whole system falls apart. In the satellite countries, the dominat issue is freedom. In Western Europe, prosperous and free, the overriding isue is peace and disarmament.

Figure 12.5: The drop shadow box after the second box is sent to the back

Manipulating Graphics

In this step you learn how to manipulate and modify both imported graphics and those created within PageMaker. Because the process of creating publications is one of constant revision, graphic manipulation skills are very important.

You can modify graphics in two basic ways: by repositioning and by resizing. We will examine these two methods and then look at two special manipulations: cropping imported graphics and wrapping text around graphics.

Repositioning Graphics

Each graphic in PageMaker, whether imported or created using a tool from the toolbox, is a distinct object that can be freely positioned on any page or on the pasteboard. To move a graphic object,

Use the arrow tool to drag graphics to new positions

1. Use the arrow tool to select the object you want to move. When the object is selected, eight handles will appear around it.

If you cannot select an object because it is covered by other objects, press the Command key while clicking at the object's location with the arrow tool. This procedure allows you to select objects that are underneath other objects.

2. Press and hold down the mouse button while pointing the arrow tool to select the object. Be sure not to position the arrow on one of the object handles. (Clicking the handles resizes the object, as you shall soon see.)

3. Keeping the mouse button down, drag the mouse to reposition the object. If you begin moving the mouse immediately after you click the mouse button, you will

see only the outline of the object as it is moved. If you hold the mouse still for a few seconds after you press the mouse button, you will see your object as you reposition it.

4. As you drag the mouse, if you reach the edge of the display and still want to drag the object further, drag into the edge. This causes PageMaker to scroll the display automatically and allows you to move your object to any point on the current page or pasteboard, regardless of the current view size.

5. Release the mouse button. The object is now in its new position. If you are unhappy with this position, you can either move the object again or choose the Undo command to move the object back to its previous position.

You can constrain the movement of any graphic as you reposition it by pressing and holding down the Shift key before you start moving the mouse. This will allow you to move only in the first direction you move your mouse: If you move horizontally, you will be prevented from moving vertically, and vice versa. Constraining your movement in this way lets you easily keep objects aligned as you move them.

Resizing Graphics

Use the arrow tool to drag the handles of any graphic you want to resize

You can easily enlarge or reduce the size of any graphic in PageMaker. You do this by selecting the object with the arrow tool and then using the arrow tool to drag one of the object's handles.

The way in which you resize the object depends on which handle you drag. Dragging one of the corner handles changes the size of the entire object, whereas dragging one of the side handles stretches the object in only one direction. Figure 13.1 shows the diagonal arrow tool that appears when you drag a corner handle.

Figure 13.1: Dragging a corner handle

You will often want to resize graphics proportionally, so that they do not become distorted. To do this, hold down the Shift key while resizing the graphic. Even if you previously distorted a graphic, holding down the Shift key while resizing it will return it to its original proportions.

When resizing scanned photographs, you can ensure that you choose an enlargement or reduction that will print at the best possible quality on your printer by using PageMaker's "magic stretch" feature. To do this,

1. Make sure your target printer is selected in the Chooser. If you will be printing to a LaserWriter or to a high-resolution imagesetter but do not have one of these devices attached to your Macintosh, select the LaserWriter driver in the Chooser anyway.

2. Choose the Print command from the File menu.

3. On the Printer pop-up menu, select the type of printer on which you will be printing your publication. (If the name of your printer type does not appear, you will have to install the proper APD files in the Aldus folder within your System folder.) Close the Print dialog box by clicking the Cancel button.

4. Select the scanned image you want to resize and hold down both the Shift and Command keys while you resize the graphic. This procedure will cause the graphic to be resized only to enlargement or reduction percentages that will allow it to retain its full resolution when it is printed on the currently selected printer.

Cropping Imported Graphics

Use the cropping tool to hide portions of an imported graphic

There is one more way to modify imported graphics. Using the cropping tool, you can "cut off" portions of any edge of your imported graphics. The cropping tool is especially useful for adjusting scanned images, which may contain more graphic information than you need to include in your publication. To crop an imported graphic,

1. Select the cropping tool from the toolbox.

2. Using the cropping tool, click the graphic you want to modify. This will cause the graphic handles to appear, just as when you select the graphic with the arrow tool.

3. Position the cropping tool so that the line through its middle is over one of the graphic handles (see Figure 13.2). Press and hold down the mouse button (the cursor will turn into a 2- or 4-headed arrow) and drag the mouse to crop the graphic.

Using the cropping tool on one of the corner handles lets you crop both horizontally and vertically. Selecting one of the side handles limits your cropping to only a single direction. After you have cropped a section of your graphic, you can

Figure 13.2: The cropping tool positioned over a graphic handle

reexpose the cropped image at any time simply by using the cropping tool again and dragging the graphic handle in the opposite direction.

After cropping a graphic, you can reposition the graphic within its new frame by positioning the cropping tool in the middle of the cropped graphic and holding down the mouse button. The cropping tool will then turn into the grabber hand tool, and moving the mouse will then move the graphic. Figure 13.3 shows this use of the grabber hand.

Wrapping Text around Graphics

The Text Wrap command, found in the Element menu, allows you to cause text blocks to automatically avoid overprinting

Figure 13.3: Using the grabber hand to reposition a cropped graphic

any independent graphic. You can specify that text jumps over a graphic, or you can specify that text wraps around all sides of the graphic. To use the Text Wrap command,

1. Select an independent graphic with the arrow tool and then choose the Text Wrap command. The Text Wrap dialog box will appear, as shown in Figure 13.4

2. Click the middle Wrap option icon. The first Wrap option icon allows text to overlay your graphic; it is used to turn off text wrapping after you have turned it on. The second icon causes text to wrap around the graphic using the measurements entered in the Stand-off options. The third Wrap icon is used for custom text wraps, but it cannot be selected in this dialog box.

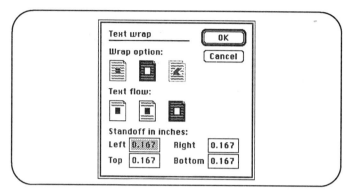

Figure 13.4: The Text Wrap dialog box

3. The Standoff option boxes specify how far text is off-set from the current graphic on the left, right, top, and bottom. You can either accept the default values or enter new values.

4. Click the OK button. Your graphic will now be sur-rounded by a thin dotted box, which is the graphic boundary around which text will wrap.

Using the arrow tool, you can customize the graphic bound-ary to cause text to wrap around any irregularly shaped ob-ject. Do this by adding additional graphic boundary handles to the graphic boundary and then positioning the graphic boundary handles so that the graphic boundary defines the ir-regular path that you want the wrapping text to follow.

The graphic boundary created by the Text Wrap command automatically has four graphic boundary handles: one at each corner. To add additional handles, select the arrow tool, se-lect the graphic by clicking it with the arrow tool, and then click the mouse button at any point on the graphic boundary. (Click the mouse button quickly; do not press down the but-ton and drag the mouse.)

After adding a new handle, point the arrow tool to the handle, press and hold the mouse button, and drag the mouse. Use this procedure to customize the graphic boundary. Release the mouse button after you have moved the handle. By repeatedly adding handles and repositioning them, you can create custom graphic boundaries, and therefore custom text wrapping, as shown in Figure 13.5.

Save Money on Airfares

With our new MajorSaver
Program, you can earn mor
any other program offers. I:
can be enjoying a new t
apron! In
will be h
& Curly
OverTheTop tennis raquet

Figure 13.5: A customized graphic boundary

In this step you learn about style sheets, perhaps the most important productivity tool in PageMaker. You may be familiar with style sheets from your word processor. If you have never used style sheets before, you certainly will find them useful in PageMaker.

Style sheets make it easy for you to use paragraph and character formats repeatedly and to ensure consistency throughout a single publication or across multiple publications. If you create long documents, or if you create the same type of document over and over again, style sheets will save you hours of effort and improve the quality of your publications.

Understanding Style Sheets

The process of applying text and paragraph formatting attributes to all of the text in a publication is essentially repetitive. After all, most publications use only three or four types of formatting, and even the most complex documents use fewer than a dozen different formats. Style sheets alleviate the repetitive nature of text formatting by letting you apply a complex set of character and paragraph formatting instructions with a single mouse click.

Style sheets help you format text paragraphs quickly and uniformly

This book, for example, uses four basic types of paragraphs: headlines, body text, lists, and figure captions. Each of these uses a unique combination of text and paragraph formats. Without using a style sheet, the formatting process for this book would require the repeated application of the appropriate text and paragraph attributes to each paragraph. This process would undoubtedly be arduous, and formatting errors likely would be made.

Using a style sheet, however, simplifies this process dramatically. We just define four styles (headlines, body text, lists, and figure captions) and apply these repeatedly. Enormous amounts of time are saved, and we ensure that each paragraph is formatted properly.

Another benefit of style sheets is that they centralize the formatting definitions and so allow paragraphs to be globally reformatted. If we decide to enlarge all the headlines in this book, for example, we can simply change the definition of our headline style to use a larger point size, and all the headline paragraphs to which the headline style has been applied will automatically be made larger.

Defining Style Sheets

Each new PageMaker publication automatically includes one style sheet with five default styles: Body Text, Caption, Headline, Subhead 1, and Subhead 2. You can use these styles as they are, modify them, or create new styles. To edit or create styles,

1. Choose the Define Styles command from the Type menu. The Define Styles dialog box, shown in Figure 14.1, will appear.

2. To edit one of the existing styles, select the name of the style you want to modify. The current attributes of this style will then appear below the scrolling window. Click the Edit button to access the Edit Style dialog box. Use the Type, Para, Tabs, and Hyph buttons to modify the options in the Type Specifications, Paragraph Specifications, Indents/Tabs, and Hyphenation dialog boxes, respectively.

3. To create a new style, click the New button, enter a name in the Name box, and then define style attributes using the Type, Para, Tabs, and Hyph buttons to modify

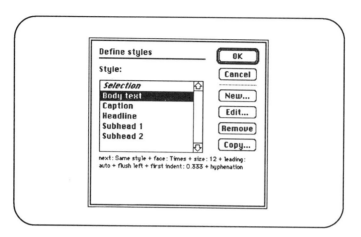

Figure 14.1: The Define Styles dialog box

the options in the Type Specifications, Paragraph Specifications, Indents/Tabs, and Hyphenation dialog boxes, respectively.

The Edit Style dialog box provides the Based On option, which makes using style sheets even easier and more productive. The Based On option allows you to give one style all of the attributes of another style as a starting point. This Based On link then remains active, and any changes made to the Based On style will automatically affect styles based on that style. If the Headline 2 style is based on the Headline 1 style, for example, and you change the font for Headline 1, Headline 2 will also use the new font (unless you specifically attribute a font to Headline 2).

Style sheets can contain type, paragraph, tab, and hyphenation information

You can also define styles by formatting an example paragraph in your publication and then creating a style using the paragraph's attributes. To do this, set the cursor in the paragraph you want to use as the style model. Then select the Define Styles command. Choose the Selection option in the Define Styles dialog box. The Edit Style dialog box will then appear, listing the formats used in the paragraph you selected. Enter a name in the Name box and click the OK button twice to complete the new style definition.

Importing Style Sheets

Rather than creating a new style sheet, it is often easier to import existing style sheets from either your word processing files or from other PageMaker publications.

Microsoft Word is the preferred word processor for PageMaker

When importing Microsoft Word files, PageMaker automatically imports all Word style sheets as well. If the Style names used in your Word document already exist in PageMaker, the PageMaker styles will be applied to the Word paragraphs.

When you use word processing software that does not support style sheets, or that uses style sheets incompatible with PageMaker, you can use style name tags to apply style sheets when you import text. A style name tag is simply the name of the style that should be applied to a specific paragraph, listed before the paragraph and enclosed in greater-than and less-than signs. Figure 14.2 shows some sample text containing style name tags.

Tags let you use style sheets with any word processor

You can insert style name tags manually before paragraphs in a word processor, or you can insert them using a macro program or glossary function. By selecting the Export Tags options in the Export dialog box, you can add style name tags to text that is exported from PageMaker.

When importing text that contains style name tags, you must select the Read Tags option at the bottom of the Place dialog box. This option instructs PageMaker to remove the tags from the text as it is imported and to apply the named styles to the text.

<ahead>Defining Colors

<para>Working with colors in PageMaker is much like working with style sheets, as described in step 14. To begin the process of defining colors to be used in your publication, choose the Define Colors command from the Element menu. This will bring up the Define Colors dialog box, as shown in Figure 16.1

<fcap>Figure 16.1: The Define Colors dialog box

<para>Each PageMaker publication automatically includes six colors; Paper, Black, Registration, Blue, Green, and Red. The first three of these colors are used by PageMaker to display the electronic pages in the publication window, and cannot be deleted. Of these, only the color Paper can be redefined. The colors Blue, Green and Red are provided simply as starter colors, and can be modified or deleted as necessary.

<nleft>You can define new colors using either of the three common color models, or by selecting a Pantone color.

Figure 14.2: Text containing style name tags

Another way to import style sheets into your publication is by copying them from other PageMaker files. You do this by choosing the Define Styles command and then clicking the Copy button in the Define Styles dialog box. Select the Page-Maker publication that contains the style sheet you want to use and click the OK button. Imported style sheets will over-write any existing style sheets, but you will be warned before any style sheets are overwritten.

Applying Styles

To use styles, open the style palette by choosing the Style Palette command from the Window menu. The style palette lists all styles currently defined in the current publication. You can resize the style palette by dragging the lower-left corner of the window, and you can reposition the palette by dragging its title bar.

To apply a style to a paragraph in your publication, set the text cursor in the paragraph and click the name of the style you want to apply. After a style has been applied, the style name is automatically selected in the palette when you place the text cursor in any paragraph.

Step 15

The Story Editor

In this step you will learn to use PageMaker's built-in word processor: the story editor. The story editor makes editing the text in your publication easy because it makes text easier to read, allows you to see a large section of text at once, and provides word processing features such as search and replace and spell checking.

Opening the Story Editor

To edit an existing story, you can access the story editor in either of two ways:

- Using the arrow tool, you can triple-click one of the text blocks in the story.

- You can select a text block with the arrow tool, or set the text tool inside a text block, and then choose the Edit Story command from the Edit menu.

When the story editor window opens, all of the text from the selected story appears in one long, scrolling window. This window includes all of the story's text, regardless of how many text blocks contain the text in the publication window. Figure 15.1 shows a sample story editor window.

You can resize and reposition story editor windows just like any other Macintosh windows, using the size box and title bar. If you use a large monitor or a dual-monitor system, you can position story editor windows so that they do not block your view of the publication window.

When you work in the story editor, PageMaker presents a slightly modified menu bar. The Element and Page menus are removed, and a new Story menu is added. Also, the Options

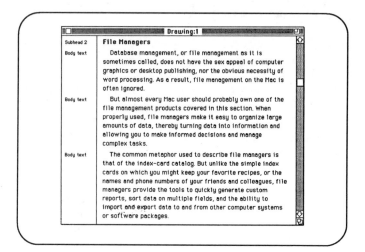

Figure 15.1: A story editor window

menu presents few commands when the story editor is active, although several Option menu commands that were dimmed in the publication window are now available.

Setting the Font and Type Size

The story editor displays all text in a single font and type size. This makes text easier to read than it is when the screen displays the varied fonts and sizes used in most layouts. You can specify the specific font and type size used in the story editor in the Preferences dialog box, accessed by choosing the Preferences command from the Edit menu.

While working in the story editor, you can apply any specific font or type size, as well as any other character attribute, to any selected text, but font or size changes will not be effective until you close the story editor and return to the publication window.

Creating New Stories

In addition to providing a convenient way to edit text that is already placed in your publication, the story editor also can be used to create new stories. You create new stories by importing text into the story editor or by using the story editor as a word processor when you write new text.

From the publication window, you can open the story editor to create or import a new story, rather than to edit an existing story. Choose the Edit Story command while no text block is selected, and while the text tool is not positioned inside of any text blocks. Once inside the story editor, you can create a new empty story window at any time by choosing the New Story command from the Story menu. After creating this new story, you can transfer it into your layout, as described here.

To import text from a word processing file into the story editor, choose the Import command from the Story menu. When you are working in the publication window, this command performs the same function as the File menu's Place command. Choosing the Import command displays the Import to Story Editor window, shown in Figure 15.2, which includes exactly the same options as the Place dialog box discussed earlier in this book.

When you are working in the story editor, you use the Place command in the File menu (sometimes labeled Replace) to transfer text from the current story editor window back into the publication layout; you don't use it to import external text or graphic files. When you are working in the story editor, you must use the Import command from the Story menu to import external files.

Importing word processing files into the story editor is an easy way to prescreen imported files when you are unsure of their content. For example, if you have a number of files with similar names and are unsure as to which one you want to use

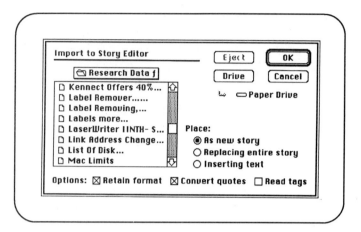

Figure 15.2: The Import to Story Editor dialog box

in your layout, use the story editor and the Import command to open the files and locate the one you want to use. You can then place the correct file in your publication and discard the unwanted files quickly and easily.

Search and Replace

In the story editor, you can search for specific text or for text that has been formatted with specific character attributes or styles. You can limit your search to a specific range of text, search an entire story, or search all text in the current publication.

1. Open a story editor window for the story you want to search.

2. Choose the Find command from the Edit menu. The Find dialog box will appear, as shown in Figure 15.3.

3. If you want to search for a specific word or phrase, enter that text into the Find What option box. Use the Match Case option if you want the capitalization of the

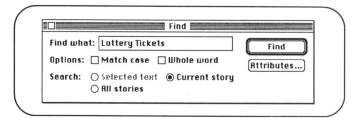

Figure 15.3: The Find dialog box

text to match exactly and use the Whole Word option to limit your search to complete matches. To specify the formatting attributes of your search, click the Attributes button and specify the Paragraph Style, Font, Size, and Type Style options to define your search.

If you specify attributes while leaving the Find What option box empty, PageMaker will find any text that uses the specified formatting. You can use this feature, for example, to locate each occurrence of a particular style or to find where you have used a specific font.

4. Specify the range of text to be searched by choosing the Selected Text, Current Story, or All Stories option. Choosing the All Stories option instructs PageMaker to search all text blocks in your entire publication.

5. Click the Find button, and the search of the selected text range will begin. When a match is found, the story editor window highlights the text that has been located. You can then close the Find dialog box or click the Find Next button to search for the next text match.

The Find Next command, on the Edit menu, allows you to repeat your most recent search without changing the options in the Find dialog box.

Using the Change command, which is also on the Edit menu, you can find and replace any text or text attributes. The Change dialog box, shown in Figure 15.4, includes all of the same options as the Find dialog box, plus the Change To option box and the Change, Change & Find, and Change All buttons.

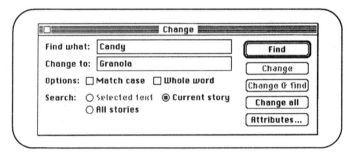

Figure 15.4: The Change dialog box

To replace one word or phrase with another, enter the text you want to locate in the Find What option box and enter the text you want substituted in the Change To option box. Click the Find button, and PageMaker will search for the specified text, highlighting it when it is found. You can then click the Change button to replace the highlighted text with the text in the Change To option box, or you can click the Change & Find button to replace the highlighted text and search for the next occurrence of the Find What text.

Clicking the Attributes button lets you specify the style, font, type size, and type style of the text you want to find and the text you want to replace. If you leave the Find What and Change To option boxes empty, PageMaker will find any text with the specified Find attributes and change the formatting to that specified by the Change attributes.

To change all underlined text in your publication to bold, choose the Change command, leave the Find What and

Change To options empty, click the All Stories option, and then click the Attributes button. Select Underline in the Find Type Style pop-up menu and select Bold in the Change To Type Style pop-up menu. Click the OK button to close the Attributes dialog box, and then click the Change All button. All underlined text in your publication will be changed to bold.

Spell Checking

PageMaker's spell-checking feature lets you check the spelling of any text selection, of an entire story, or of all text in the current publication. Suggested replacement spellings are automatically offered for unknown words, and you can add new words to your own dictionary so that they are not flagged as unknown in the future.

1. Open the story editor and a story editor window that contains some or all of the text you want to check.

2. If you want to spell check only a small section of your text, highlight this section by dragging the text cursor over it.

3. Choose the Spelling command from the Edit menu.

4. If you want to spell check only the currently selected text, choose the Selected Text option. If you want to spell check the text in the current story only, choose the Current Story option. To spell check all of the text in every story in the current publication, choose the All Stories option.

5. Click the Start button. PageMaker will begin to scan the selected text for misspelled words. When the program finds an unknown word, it displays the word along with a list of suggested corrections, as shown in Figure 15.5.

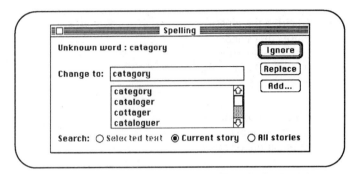

Figure 15.5: The Spelling dialog box making a suggestion

6. If the unknown word is spelled correctly, click the Ignore button to leave it unchanged or click the Add button to add that word to your dictionary so that it is not considered unknown in future sessions.

    To replace the unknown word with one of the suggested words, select the word in the suggestion list that you want to use and click the Replace button. You can also correct the word by editing it in the Change To option box and then clicking the Replace button.

    After you click the Ignore or Replace button, Page-Maker continues to check the spelling of the remaining text.

7. After all of your text has been checked, or at any time during the spell-checking process, you can close the Spelling dialog box by clicking the close box in the title bar.

Closing the Story Editor

When you are done editing text in the story editor, you can close the story editor windows and return to the publication window in several ways.

- Clicking the close box in any story editor window closes that window. If you click the close box of the last, or only, story editor window, you are returned to the publication window. Clicking the close box of a story that has not already been placed in the layout displays the Story Has Not Been Placed dialog box (see Figure 15.6), where you can choose to discard the text in that window, add the text in that window to your publication, or cancel the closing operation.

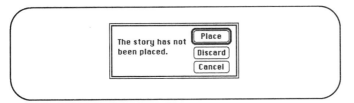

Figure 15.6: The Story Has Not Been Placed dialog box

- Choosing the Close Story command from the Story menu has the same effect as clicking the close box in the current story window.

- To close any story editor window and add the edited text from that window to the current layout, choose the Place or Replace command from the File menu. This command will appear as *Place* only when the story being editing has not already been positioned in the current layout (if it was newly created or imported). After you choose the Place command, you will be returned to the publication window, and a text place-ment cursor will appear, allowing you to flow the text into your layout.

Choosing the Replace command has the same effect as click-ing the close box in a story editor window. Edited text from a story that has already been placed is always automatically added to the publication.

- To return to the publication window without closing any of the current story editor windows, choose the Edit Layout command from the Edit menu.

- You can also return to the publication window, or bring any story editor window to the front, by choosing the window title from the Window menu. In addition, you can use the Window menu to return to the story editor from the publication window.

This step introduces the ways in which you can use color in your PageMaker publications. PageMaker supports both spot colors and process colors, so you can create documents that can be reproduced using either spot-color printing techniques or four-color-process printing techniques.

You can take advantage of PageMaker's color features even if you are working on a black-and-white Macintosh system. Any color information you specify will be stored in the file and will print properly either to a color printer or as color separations.

Defining Colors

Working with colors in PageMaker is much like working with style sheets, as described in Step 14. To begin the process of defining colors to be used in your publication, choose the Define Colors command from the Element menu. The Define Colors dialog box will appear, as shown in Figure 16.1

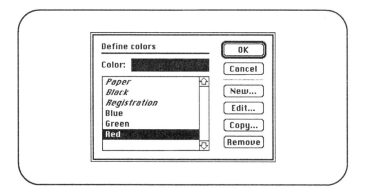

Figure 16.1: The Define Colors dialog box

Each PageMaker publication automatically includes six Define Colors options: Paper, Black, Registration, Blue, Green, and Red. The first three are used by PageMaker to display the electronic pages in the publication window and cannot be deleted. Of these three, only Paper can be redefined. The colors Blue, Green, and Red are provided simply as starter colors and can be modified or deleted as necessary.

You can define new colors using any of the three common color models or by selecting a Pantone color

To define a new color, click the New button. The Edit Color dialog box will appear, as shown in Figure 16.2. This dialog box allows you to define (or edit) a color using either of the three popular color models—Red Green Blue, Hue Lightness Saturation, or Cyan Magenta Yellow Black—or to pick a color from the Pantone color library.

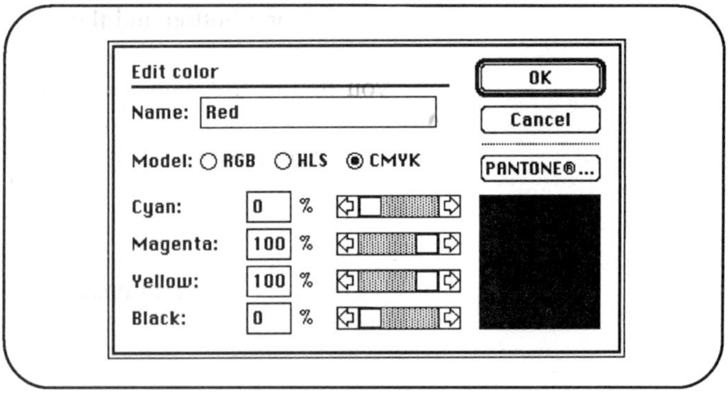

Figure 16.2: The Edit Color dialog box

To begin defining a new color, select a color model by using the Model option radio buttons, or click the Pantone button, select a color from the scrolling color list, and click the OK button to close the Pantone dialog box. Edit your color either by entering values into the color-component option boxes or by manipulating the horizontal scroll bars that appear next to each color component. If you are working on a color monitor, the color you have created will appear to the right of the color-component options.

When you are satisfied with your new color, enter a name for the color in the Name option box. Your color name can include up to 32 characters, although some special characters cannot be used in color names. When you are satisfied with your color name and definition, click the OK button to return to the Define Colors dialog box.

You can now continue to define new colors, or you can edit any of the existing colors by selecting their names and clicking the Edit button. This will reopen the Edit Colors dialog box, where you can modify the selected color by manipulating the color component definitions.

From the Define Colors dialog box, you can also import colors that have been created and stored in another PageMaker publication. To do this, click the Copy button and then select the PageMaker file that contains the colors you want to import. If any of the colors you import use names identical to those already defined, a dialog box will appear warning you that the imported colors will replace those currently defined.

Storing all of your frequently used colors in a single Page-Maker publication and using the Copy button to import them into any publication you create saves time and ensures consistency among your publications

Applying Colors

The first step in using colors in your publication is to display the color palette (see Figure 16.3). To do this, choose the Color Palette option from the Windows menu. Like other palettes, you can resize the color palette, and you can reposition it by dragging its title bar.

To apply a specific color to text in your publication, select the text with the text tool and then choose the color you want to apply from the color palette. You can also select the color you

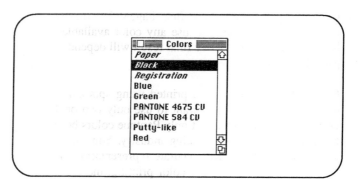

Figure 16.3: The Color menu

want to apply using the Color option pop-up menu in the Type Specifications dialog box.

If you are using a style sheet to format your text, define a color for the style sheet using the Color option in the Type Specification dialog box.

To apply a color to a graphic element, select the graphic element with the arrow tool and then, on the color palette, click the name of the color you want to apply.

To quickly edit the definition of any color, hold down the Command key and click the color name on the color palette. The Edit Color dialog box will appear, where you can modify the definition of the color.

Color and the Printing Process

When deciding which colors to use in your publication, keep in mind the type of printer on which your publication will ultimately be printed and the reproduction method that will be used to duplicate your final prints.

If you will be printing your final PageMaker files to a color PostScript printer, you can use any color available in Page-Maker. The quality of your final result will depend on the capabilities of the color printer.

If your publication will be printed using spot-color printing techniques, you probably want to use only two or three colors. You may want to select only Pantone colors because they are widely used in the printing industry. Your on-screen design will provide a fairly accurate representation of the final results. When you use spot-color printing, the specific color used to represent a spot color on the screen does not really matter; you could use the default colors of red and blue on the screen, print your separations, and then instruct your printer to use any two colors in the actual printing process.

If your publication will be output to four-color-process separations and printed using a four-color-process printing technique, you are free to use as many on-screen colors as you like, but you must pay careful attention to your color selection as it will directly affect your final printed publications. Producing four-color-process publications requires you to keep your color monitor calibrated, work with a color service bureau that knows how to produce accurate separations from PageMaker, and select a printer who has experience working with desktop-produced separations.

Importing Color Graphics

Using the Place command, you can import color TIFF, EPS (encapsulated PostScript files) PICT, and MPNT (MacPaint) files into PageMaker. These files will appear in color in Page-Maker using the full spectrum of colors available on your system.

Imported color graphics will usually print along with the black separation when you produce spot-color separations directly from PageMaker. Using Aldus PrePrint, a process-color separation utility sold separately, you can separate color EPS and TIFF files for four-color-process printing along with your entire PageMaker publication.

Step 17

Printing

This step describes the process of printing PageMaker files to PostScript-equipped laser printers. PageMaker provides a wide range of printing options, allowing you to control enlargement and reduction, crop marks, spot-color separations, font downloading, and much more.

Using the Chooser

As in other Macintosh applications, you should use the Chooser desk accessory to select your target printer before you choose the Print command from the File menu. This procedure is especially important when you are working in PageMaker, because the dialog box displayed when you choose the Print command depends on the type of printer currently selected in the Chooser.

For the best possible results, you should use a PostScript laser printer when working with PageMaker. For the remainder of this step, we will assume that you have selected the Laser-Writer icon in your Chooser. If you have selected some other type of printing device, the printing dialog boxes and options will vary slightly from those described here.

The Print Dialog Box

To begin the process of printing your publication, choose the Print command from the File menu. The Print To dialog box, shown in Figure 17.1, will then appear. The name of the specific printer currently selected in the Chooser will appear on the top line of this dialog box.

Most of the options presented in the upper portion of this dialog box should be familiar to you from other Macintosh applications. The last few options, however, are unique to PageMaker.

To print a copy quickly, set only the Page Range and Printer options and then click the OK button

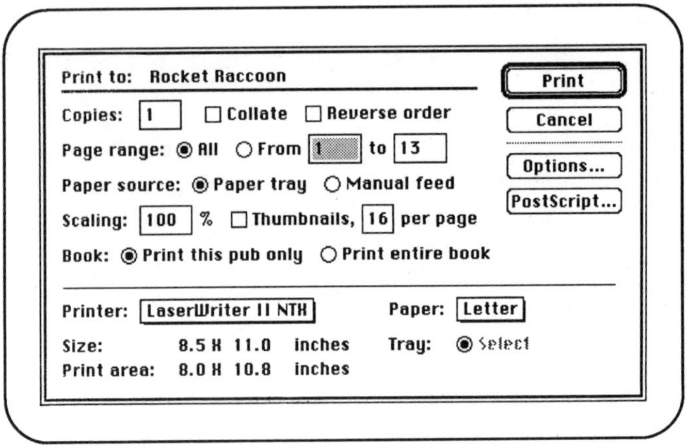

```
┌─────────────────────────────────────────────────────────────┐
│  Print to:  Rocket Raccoon                    ┌──────────┐   │
│                                                │  Print   │   │
│  Copies:  │1│    ☐ Collate  ☐ Reverse order   └──────────┘   │
│                                                ┌──────────┐   │
│  Page range: ◉ All  ○ From │1│ to │13│         │  Cancel  │   │
│                                                └──────────┘   │
│  Paper source: ◉ Paper tray  ○ Manual feed   ┌ Options... ┐  │
│                                                              │
│  Scaling: │100│ %  ☐ Thumbnails, │16│ per page │PostScript...││
│                                                              │
│  Book: ◉ Print this pub only  ○ Print entire book            │
│  ─────────────────────────────────────────────────────────  │
│  Printer: │LaserWriter II NTH│       Paper: │Letter│         │
│  Size:       8.5 H 11.0  inches      Tray:  ◉ Select         │
│  Print area: 8.0 H 10.8  inches                              │
└─────────────────────────────────────────────────────────────┘
```

Figure 17.1: The Print To dialog box

Use the Scaling option to reduce the pages of your publication to 25 to 99 percent of normal size, or to enlarge pages by 101 to 1000 percent. If your enlarged pages are bigger than the paper on which you are printing, you will want to use the Tile option, found in the Aldus Print Options dialog box, described later in this step.

Use the Thumbnails option to print pages that contain miniature versions of several publication pages on a single page. You can control the number of miniature pages printed with the Thumbnails option by entering a value between 2 and 64 for the Per Page option.

The Print To dialog box provides two Book commands: Print This Pub Only and Print Entire Book. These commands are available only if you used the Book command to define a list of PageMaker publications that are related to the current publication. The Print This Pub Only option limits your printing to the current PageMaker file. Selecting the Print Entire Book option instructs PageMaker to print every file in the Book dialog box book list when you click the Print dialog box OK button.

Use the Printer command pop-up menu to select the specific printer type on which you will be printing. The printer names in this list are those for which APD files were installed during PageMaker installation. Figure 17.2 shows a sample Printer command pop-up menu.

General
AST TurboLaser/PS
Color General
LaserWriter II NT
✓LaserWriter II NTX
LaserWriter Plus
Linotronic 100/300
Linotronic 500
QMS ColorScript 100
Silentwriter

Figure 17.2: The Printer command pop-up menu

After selecting your printer name, choose a paper size using the Paper option. Then confirm that the dimensions displayed next to the Size and Print Area options are correct.

If you need to add more printers to your pop-up menu, copy the required APD files from your original PageMaker disks into the APD folder, located in the Aldus folder within your System folder.

After setting the options in the Print To dialog box, you can click the OK button to begin the printing process, click the Options button to modify the Aldus print options (described next), click the PostScript button to modify the PostScript printing options (described later in this step), or click the Cancel button to return to the publication window without printing.

The Aldus Print Options Dialog Box

Clicking the Options button in the Print To dialog box displays the Aldus Print Options dialog, shown in Figure 17.3.

```
┌─────────────────────────────────────────────┐
│  Aldus print options              ┌───OK───┐ │
│                                   └─────────┘ │
│  ☒ Proof print      ☒ Crop marks  ┌─Cancel─┐ │
│  ☐ Substitute fonts ☐ Smooth      └────────┘ │
│  ☒ Spot color overlays: │All colors│         │
│  ☐ Knockouts                                 │
│  ☐ Tile: ○ Manual   ⦿ Auto overlap│0.65│ inches │
│  ☐ Print blank pages                         │
│                                              │
│  Even/odd pages: ⦿ Both  ○ Even  ○ Odd       │
│  Orientation: ⦿ Tall ○ Wide   Image: ☐ Invert ☐ Mirror │
└─────────────────────────────────────────────┘
```

Figure 17.3: The Aldus Print Options dialog box

Use the Proof Print option to speed up PageMaker printing

The Proof Print option instructs PageMaker to replace each imported graphic in printed publications with a box containing an X. This replacement allows your pages to print much more quickly.

If your publication includes color, you may want to use the Spot Color Overlays and Knockouts options. Use the Spot Color Overlays option to instruct PageMaker to print one or more of the colors that have been applied to text or graphic elements on separate pages. Using the adjoining pop-up menu, you can choose to print spot-color separations for all colors in the publication or for only one specific color.

When printing spot-color separations, use the Crop Marks option to print special alignment marks and the name of each separation color on each separation.

When creating spot-color separations, you can use the Knockouts option to avoid the problems associated with inks mixing during the printing process. When you use the Knock-outs option, portions of text or graphic elements that are over-lapped by other text or graphic elements are eliminated from the separations. Eliminating these elements allows the over-printing text or graphic element to be applied directly to the paper, avoiding the problems associated with applying one ink directly on top of another.

Use the Tile option when printing publication pages that are larger than the paper on which they are being printed. In most cases, you will want to use the Auto Overlap tiling option, which automatically calculates where to position page breaks.

When you are done manipulating the options in the Al-dus Print Options dialog box, click the OK button to return to the Print To dialog box.

The PostScript Print Options dialog box

To access the PostScript Print Options dialog box, shown in Figure 17.4, click the PostScript button in the Print To dialog box. This dialog box includes a number of useful options.

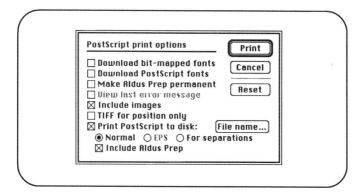

Figure 17.4: The PostScript Print Options dialog box

The Download Bit-Mapped Fonts and Download PostScript Fonts options control whether or not these fonts are automatically transferred to your printer as needed. When PageMaker automatically downloads fonts, the Printer Status dialog box informs you of each font being downloaded, as shown in Figure 17.5.

Downloading PostScript® font: ItcEras-Bold.

Font Melior is not found on LaserWriter Plus, substituting Courier.

Figure 17.5: Two sample Printer Status dialog boxes

Use the TIFF for Position Only option to output only low-resolution versions of your imported TIFF files. This option saves time when you are printing proof copies of your files. Deselect this option when printing final pages or color separations.

Use the Print PostScript to Disk option to create PostScript files: to transfer files to a service bureau for high-resolution output, to create an EPS file of a single PageMaker page that can then be used as a PageMaker graphic or by another software application, or to prepare separation files for Aldus Pre-Print or another four-color separation utility.

1. To create a PostScript file, select the Print PostScript to Disk option.

2. Choose the type of PostScript file you want to create by clicking the Normal, EPS, or For Separation radio button.

3. Click the File Name button to specify the file name and location of the PostScript file you will create.

4. When creating Normal PostScript files, click the Include Aldus Prep option if your service bureau has instructed you to do so. In most cases, you will not need to select this option.

5. Click the OK button to begin creating a PostScript file. The file will be saved with the name and location you specified.

This step introduces two advanced PageMaker features: indexing and table of contents generation. You will use these features most often when you create long documents consisting of several PageMaker publication files, such as books or manuals. Used properly, these features eliminate hours or even days of manual effort and make your publications more useful to their readers.

The Book Command

When working with documents that include more than one PageMaker file, you must use the Book command to create a logical relationship between the files before you create an index or table of contents.

1. Open the PageMaker file in which you want to position your index or table of contents.

2. Choose the Book command from the File menu. The Book Publication List dialog box, shown in Figure 18.1, will appear.

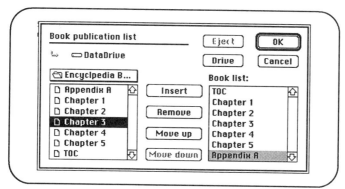

Figure 18.1: The Book Publication List dialog box

Often you will want to create one new publication file for your index and another new file for your table of contents. You will have to use the Book command in each file.

3. The Book Publication List dialog box is used much like the Apple Font/DA Mover. In the left window, select the name of the first PageMaker file that will appear in your publication and click the Insert button. This file name will then be added to the Book List window. Repeat this procedure, adding each of the files that are part of the final publication, until the Book List window contains the names of all the files you want included in your index or table of contents.

4. Click the OK button to close the dialog box. You are now ready to create your index or table of contents.

Marking Index Entries

To include a word or phrase in your index, you must mark the word or phrase each time it appears in your publications and then specify the reference that will appear in the index. Page-Maker refers to each word or phrase in your index as a topic reference. Topic references can contain up to 50 characters.

To include text as a topic reference, select the text with the text tool and then choose the Index Entry command from the Options menu. This will bring up the Create Index Entry dialog box, shown in Figure 18.2. This dialog box is used to edit the topic reference text and to specify the range of pages to which the index reference refers.

The text you selected when you chose the Create Index Entry command appears in the first Topic option box. You can edit this text, if necessary. If you cannot see all of the text, use the arrow keys to scroll right or left within the option box.

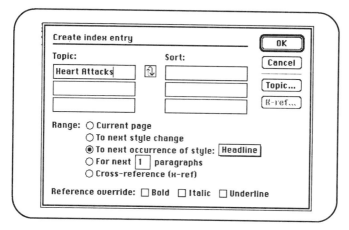

Figure 18.2: The Create Index Entry dialog box

If you have already created index entries for this topic, either in the current file or in other files on your book list, you can verify the spelling or terminology of the index entry by clicking the Topic button and locating the existing entries in alphabetical lists.

The Range option you select determines the listing that appears for the topic reference when it appears in the index. Five range options are available;

- The Current Page option causes the page number on which the topic reference appears to be listed in the index.

- The To Next Style Change option lists the range of pages starting with the page on which the topic reference appears and ending with the page that contains the first paragraph after the topic reference that uses a different style sheet. This option is most often used to specify a range of pages ending with the next headline or subhead.

- The To Next Occurrence of Style option is similar to the To Next Style Change option. You select a specific style sheet, and when this style sheet occurs, the page range ends.

- The For Next ___ Paragraphs option lists a range of pages starting with the page on which the topic reference appears and ending with the page that contains the nth paragraph, where n is a value specified in the option box.

- The Cross Reference option directs inquiries regarding one index entry to another index entry. For example, a book about boxing might have many indexed references to Muhammad Ali. You could use the Cross Reference option to direct readers who look up ''Cassius Clay'' to the Muhammad Ali references. Use the X-ref button to select a specific cross-reference topic.

Click the OK button to close the Create Index Entry dialog box. If you are using the story editor, a small black diamond will appear before the text you have selected as your topic reference.

You can quickly create an index entry by selecting text and then pressing Shift-Command-; (semicolon). This procedure lets you index the selected text without opening the Create Index Entry dialog box, using the default Range option.

Editing Index Entries

To edit a single index entry, open a story editor window that contains your indexed text. Select the black diamond that appears in front of the index entry you want to modify and choose the Create Index Entry command. The Create Index Entry dialog box will appear, and you can then modify any aspects of the selected index entry.

To review all of the index entries you have made in the current publication, or in all publications that will be part of your index, choose the Show Index command from the Options menu. The Show Index dialog box, shown in Figure 18.3, will then appear. If you have used the Book command to define the publications included in your final document, this dialog box will include all index entries from all publications.

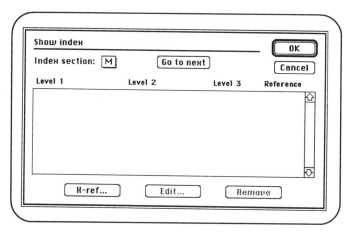

Figure 18.3: The Show Index dialog box

The Show Index dialog box lists, for one letter of the alphabet at a time, each index entry and the assigned reference. To move between letters of the alphabet, use the Index Section pop-up menu or click the Go to Next button. To modify a specific entry, select it with the arrow tool and then click the Edit button. You can then change any of the options in the Create Index Entry dialog box.

Generating an Index

Once you have defined and edited your index entries, you are ready to compile and place your index. Open the publication file in which you want to lay out your index, verify that the

Book command has been used to specify all related publications, and then choose the Create Index command from the Options menu. The Create Index dialog box, shown in Figure 18.4, will then appear.

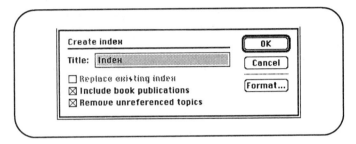

Figure 18.4: The Create Index dialog box

If this is the first time you have created an index for the current publication, click the OK button. PageMaker will then compile your index. If you are using the layout view, a text placement icon will appear, and your new index can then be positioned just like any other imported story. If you are using the story editor when you choose the Create Index command, a new story window will appear, which you can then place into your publication by choosing the Place command from the File menu.

Once your index is in position, you can freely edit the text in your index. Remember, however, that if you later reindex your publication, all of your text edits will be overwritten by the new index.

Creating a Table of Contents

For PageMaker to create a table of contents for your publication, you must first mark each paragraph—which usually will be a heading or subheading—that should be included. Do this by placing the text cursor in the paragraph you want to mark, choosing the Paragraph command from the Type menu, and then selecting the Include in Table of Contents option.

If you use style sheets to format your long documents, as you likely will, you can usually mark all the paragraphs that should be included in your table of contents by selecting the Include in Table of Contents option in the paragraph definition for your headlines and subheads.

After you mark your paragraphs, you are ready to generate the table of contents. To begin, open the file in which the table of contents will be laid out and confirm that all associated publications are listed in the Book Publication List dialog box. Next, choose the Create TOC command from the Options menu. The Create Table of Contents dialog box will then appear. If necessary, modify the options in this dialog box. Then click the OK button.

If you are working in the publication window, a text placement icon will appear. Place the text as you would any imported story. (If you are working in the story editor, a new story window containing the table of contents will be opened.) The table of contents story will include the complete text of all marked paragraphs, plus the number of the page on which each paragraph appears.

Once the table of contents is placed, you can edit or format the table of contents text as required. As with indexes, any editing performed on the table of contents will be lost if you later generate a new table of contents. For this reason, it is best not to edit the table of contents until all publication changes that affect final page numbering are complete and the table of contents is re-created.

PageMaker automatically creates styles on the style sheet to format the table of contents, and you can modify the table of contents formatting by editing this style sheet.

This step introduces powerful file management commands that you can use to manually or automatically update imported text or graphics files. These commands are useful for publications being created in workgroup situations, and for publications that are regularly updated, such as price lists and brochures.

Understanding Links

When you import a text or graphics file into PageMaker, you normally keep a copy of the file as part of your publication file. But suppose you (or someone else) modifies the original text or graphics file, and you want to bring that updated file into your PageMaker publication. PageMaker's link management commands allow you to control whether and when updated versions of your text and graphics files are used in your publications.

The Links Command

To experiment with the Links command, open a publication file that includes several imported text and graphics. Choose the Links command from the File menu. The Links dialog box, shown in Figure 19.1, will appear.

The Links dialog box lists each imported file along with the page number on which it appears and the current link status. Five different link status conditions exist, each of which is indicated by a specific character or icon that appears before the file name. In addition, selecting a particular element displays the current link status below the scrolling element

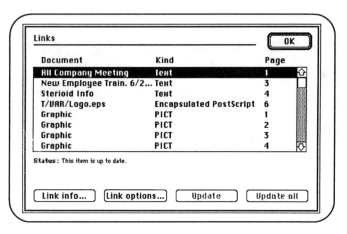

Figure 19.1: The Links dialog box

window. The link symbols are as follows:

- No symbol. Either the external file has not been modified since it was imported, or no link exists for this element.

- Question mark. PageMaker is unable to locate the external file. You can reestablish this link, as described later in this chapter.

- Solid black diamond. The external file has been modified since it was imported, and this element will be updated automatically the next time your publication is opened or printed or when you press the Update button.

- Open diamond. The external file has been modified, but the element is not set for updating. To update the link, press the Update button.

- Open triangle. The external file has been modified, and the version of the file currently in the publication also has been modified.

Below the scrolling element list are four buttons: Link Info, Link Options, Update, and Update All. The Link Info button performs exactly like the Link Info command, described in the next section. The Link Options command brings up the Link Options dialog box, which controls whether copies of the linked element are stored in the publication file, and whether updated elements are imported automatically.

The Update button replaces the current version of the selected element with the version currently stored in the linked file. The Update All button replaces all elements with updated versions from the linked files.

The Link Info Command

To verify or modify the link status of any particular text or graphic element in your publication, select the element with the arrow tool and choose the Link Info command on the Element menu. The Link Info dialog box, shown in Figure 19.2, will then appear.

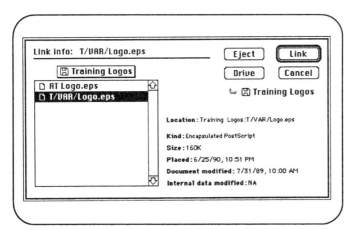

Figure 19.2: The Link Info dialog box

The scrolling file list at the left side of this dialog box in most cases displays the folder and file to which the selected element is currently linked. The right side of the dialog box provides information about the linked file, including the date and time it was placed in PageMaker and the date and time that the disk file was last modified.

To update or modify the link, select from the scrolling list the name of the file you want to link. Then click the Link button. You can link either an updated version of the original file or an entirely different file. The contents of the newly linked file will replace the previously linked file in your publication.

The Link Options Command

You can use the Link Options command in two different ways. If you select the Link Options command when you have selected no specific element, the Link Options: Defaults dialog box appears, as shown in Figure 19.3.

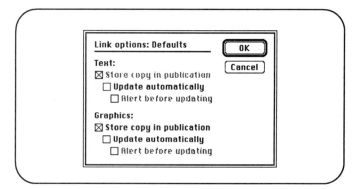

Figure 19.3: The Link Options: Defaults dialog box

This dialog box presents three options for text elements and three options for graphics elements. The Store Copy in Publication option determines whether imported files are copied into the PageMaker file or accessed directly from the external disk file. You cannot turn off this option for text files; they must be stored in the publication. When you select the Update Automatically option, PageMaker accesses the most recent version of your text or graphics files each time you open or print your publication. If you select the Alert before Updating option, you will be warned before any automatic updates occur so that you can cancel or acknowledge them.

If you select the Link Options command after you choose a specific text or graphics element, the Link Options dialog box appears, as shown in Figure 19.4. This dialog box presents the same options as the Link Options: Defaults dialog box, but these options affect only the selected text or graphics element.

You can save considerable disk space by not storing large graphics files in your publications. Whenever you do store graphics files, however, keep careful records of the external graphics files, as you will need them each time you open or print your publication.

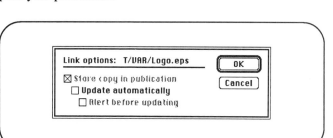

Figure 19.4: The Link Options dialog box

This step introduces the Aldus Table Editor, a separate utility program that is included along with Aldus PageMaker. The Aldus Table Editor is a specialized tool that helps you easily create complex text tables, which you can then transfer into PageMaker.

The Aldus Table Editor is automatically installed in the same folder as your Aldus PageMaker 4.0 application during installation.

Creating a New Table

After launching the Aldus Table Editor, select the New command from the File menu. The Table Setup dialog box will appear, as shown in Figure 20.1. Enter the number of columns and rows you will require in your table, the total size of the table you want to create, and the gutter space between table text and cell borders. Click the OK button, and your new table will be created.

```
Table setup                        [  OK  ]

Number of columns: [ 6    ]        [ Cancel ]

Number of rows:    [ 9    ]

Table size: [ 4    ]  by [ 5    ]  inches

Gutter in inches:    Column: [ 0.1 ]

                     Row:    [ 0.1 ]
```

Figure 20.1: The Table Setup dialog box

Entering Data into the Table

You can enter text directly into your table from the keyboard, or you can import data from any text or tab-delimited file.

To enter text into any cell in your table, select the text tool from the Table Editor toolbox and click the mouse button when the cursor is in the desired cell. Type the desired data into the cell. Press the Tab key to move one cell to the right (or to the first cell in the next row). Press the Return key to move one cell down (or to the first cell in the next column).

To import data from a text file, choose the Import command from the File menu and select the file you want to import. Choose the Replacing Entire Table option if you want the imported data to overwrite any existing data in your table. Choose the Into Selected Range option to place the imported text into specific cells.

Most spreadsheets allow you to save data in text or tab-delimited format so that you can transfer it into the Aldus Table Editor.

Formatting Tables

The Aldus Table Editor provides a number of commands that allow you to customize your table. A few of these are described here.

- To change the width of a column or the height of a row, position the cursor on the line between the column or row labels (the cursor will turn into a two-headed arrow), press the mouse button, and resize the column or row.

    Alternatively, you can select a row or column and use the Column Width or Row Height commands from the Cell menu.

- To add borders to any cell, select the cell or cells to which you want to add borders and choose the Borders command from the Cell menu. The Borders dialog box will appear, as shown in Figure 20.2.

- To format the digits in any cell that contains numbers, select the cell or the row or column that contains the numbers. Then choose the Number Format command from the Cell menu. The Number Format dialog box, shown in Figure 20.3, will appear. Choose the numbering format you want applied to the selected numbers.

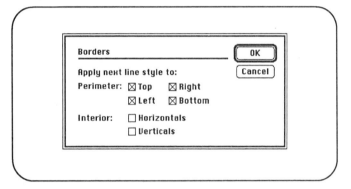

Figure 20.2: The Borders dialog box

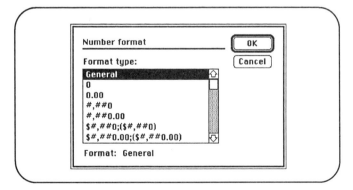

Figure 20.3: The Number Format dialog box

- To add any numbers together, select the cells that contain the numbers and choose the Sum command from the Cell menu. The addition cursor will then appear. Click the cell that you want to contain the sum.

- Use the commands in the Type, Lines, and Shades menu to modify the text formatting, border, and fill pattern of any selected cells.

Saving and Exporting

You can save files created in the Aldus Table Editor by using the Save and Save As commands. However, files saved in this manner cannot be imported to PageMaker or used by any other application.

To save tables in a format that can be used in PageMaker, you must save them in a special format using the Export command.

1. Choose the Export command from the File menu. The Export to File dialog box, shown in Figure 20.4, will appear.

   You can save files in either PICT or Text Only format if you want to import them into PageMaker. Use the PICT format if you want your table to retain all of its formatting. The only limitation of the PICT format is that you will not be able to edit the table in PageMaker. If you save the table in the Text Only format, you will lose your table formatting, but you will be able to modify the table in PageMaker.

2. Choose either the Entire Table or the Selected Cell Range option to determine which section of the current table you want to save. In most cases, you will want to save the entire table.

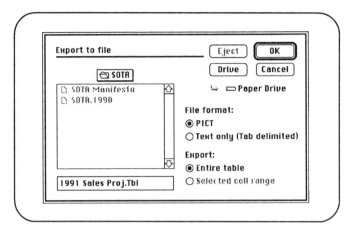

Figure 20.4: The Export to File dialog box

3. Enter a name for your file, use the Drive button and the Folder bar to choose a location for your file, and click the OK button.

4. Open the PageMaker publication into which you want to import the table. Then choose the Place command. Select the table file you saved and click the OK button.

Index